Chemistry Matters!

ORGANIC CHEMISTRY

Volume 8

Martin Clowes

an imprint of

www.scholastic.com/librarypublishing

About this set

Chemistry Matters! provides an intelligent and stimulating introduction to all areas of modern chemistry as reflected in current middle school and high school curricula. This highly visual set clearly explains principles and applications using dramatic photography and annotated artwork. Carefully chosen examples make the topic fun and relevant to everyday life. Panels detail key terms, people, events, discoveries, and technologies, and include "Try This" features, in which readers are encouraged to discover principles for themselves in safe step-by-step experiments at home or school. "Chemistry in Action" boxes give everyday examples of chemical applications.

First published in 2007 by Grolier, an imprint of
Scholastic Library Publishing
Old Sherman Turnpike
Danbury, Connecticut 06816

Volume ISBN 0-7172-6202-2; 978-0-7172-6202-1
Set ISBN 0-7172-6194-8; 978-0-7172-6194-9

Library of Congress Cataloging-in-Publication Data
Chemistry matters!
   v. cm.
   Includes bibliographical references and index.
   Contents: v.1. Atoms and molecules—v.2. States of matter—v.3. Chemical reactions—v.4. Energy and reactions—v.5. The periodic table—v.6. Metals and metalloids—v.7. Nonmetals—v.8. Organic chemistry—v.9. Biochemistry—v.10. Chemistry in action.
   ISBN 0-7172-6194-8 (set : alk. paper)—ISBN 0-7172-6195-6 (v.1 : alk. paper)—ISBN 0-7172-6196-4 (v.2 : alk. paper)—ISBN 0-7172-6197-2 (v.3 : alk. paper)—ISBN 0-7172-6198-0 (v.4 : alk. paper)—ISBN 0-7172-6199-9 (v.5 : alk. paper)—ISBN 0-7172-6200-6 (v.6 : alk. paper)—ISBN 0-7172-6201-4 (v.7 : alk. paper)—ISBN 0-7172-6202-2 (v.8 : alk. paper)—ISBN 0-7172-6203-0 (v.9 : alk. paper)—ISBN 0-7172-6204-9 (v.10 : alk. paper)
   1. Chemistry—Encyclopedias.
   QD4.C485 2007
   540—dc22
                                        2006026209

For The Brown Reference Group plc
Project Editor: Wendy Horobin
Editors: Tom Jackson, Paul Thompson,
            Susan Watt, Tim Harris
Designer: Graham Curd
Picture Researchers: Laila Torsun, Helen Simm
Illustrators: Darren Awuah, Mark Walker
Indexer: Ann Barrett
Design Manager: Sarah Williams
Managing Editor: Bridget Giles
Production Director: Alastair Gourlay
Editorial Director: Lindsey Lowe
Children's Publisher: Anne O'Daly

Academic Consultants:
Dr. Donald Franceschetti, Dept. of Physics,
   University of Memphis
Dr. Richard Petersen, Dept. of Chemistry,
   University of Memphis

Printed and bound in Singapore.

Contents

What Is Organic Chemistry?

Chemists divide chemicals into two groups: organic and inorganic. Organic chemicals contain large amounts of carbon. They occur in everything from plastics to gasoline to drugs and even make up life-forms, including you!

When you are learning about chemistry, you are shown many examples of how atoms and molecules (atoms joined together) react with each other, and how their structures affect the way they behave. Most of these examples are very simple, so you can understand them easily. You learn about water, salt, and metals—substances that you come across everyday. However, most of the substances around you now are not so simple to make or easy to understand.

COMPLEX CHEMICALS

Living bodies—the most complex things in nature—and many of the most useful materials made by people, such as plastics, fuels, and drugs, are made from

A colorful pattern is made when light shines on a layer of oil floating on water. Oil is an organic substance.

Key Terms

• **Atom:** The smallest piece of an element that still retains the properties of that element.
• **Compound:** A substance formed when atoms of two or more different elements bond together.
• **Molecule:** Two or more atoms connected by chemical bonds.

History

Dividing chemistry

Chemists first studied organic compounds in the early 19th century, when people began investigating the substances inside the bodies of life-forms. Many believed that these compounds were so complex that they could only be made inside a living body, or organism. Because of this, Swedish chemist Jöns Jacob Berzelius (1779–1848) called the compounds *organic*. All other compounds were therefore *inorganic*. However, in 1828, the German chemist Friedrich Wöhler (1800–1882) showed that organic compounds could be made in a laboratory as well. He reacted two inorganic compounds together and, completely by accident, produced urea, a substance that occurs in urine. This discovery showed that organic compounds were built the same way as other compounds, but that they were just more complicated.

◄ *Jöns Jacob Berzelius, the first organic chemist, at work in his laboratory. Berzelius also came up with the system of chemical symbols used today.*

very complex compounds. Chemists describe the compounds as being organic. That is because those compounds that occur in nature have all originally been produced by living things (*see* box above).

A compound is a substance that is made when the atoms of two or more elements bond together. Organic compounds contain many atoms, perhaps hundreds of thousands,

▶ *Coal is a rock that contains organic chemicals. Coal is used mainly as a fuel, but it is also a source of useful chemicals.*

bonded together in a very precise pattern. All organic compounds are based on the element carbon (C). The compounds also contain atoms of other elements, most often hydrogen (H), but oxygen (O), nitrogen (N), and chlorine (Cl) are also commonly involved.

CONNECTING SECTIONS

The first chemists to investigate organic compounds could not figure out much about them. The methods used for studying inorganic compounds did not work very well with organic ones. Chemists knew that organic compounds contained carbon and hydrogen because when the compounds burned, they produced water vapor (H_2O) and carbon dioxide (CO_2). Burning, or combustion,

▼ *A pair of butterflies in the wild. Their bodies are made up of organic chemicals, such as sugars, proteins, and fats. All life on Earth is based on organic compounds.*

Chemistry in Action

Chemistry and life

Chemical reactions keep all life-forms alive. It is chemical reactions that extract energy from food, cause muscles to move, build new body tissues as we grow, and repair the damaged parts. The chemistry of life involves organic compounds. These compounds are very complex to make, and understanding how they react is a science in itself, known as biochemistry (*see* vol. 9).

Many of the organic compounds produced by living things will be familiar to you. They include sugars, fats, and proteins. Sugars belong to a group of compounds called carbohydrates. They are all made up of carbon, hydrogen, and oxygen. Fats are slightly more complex molecules with long chains of joined carbon atoms. Sugars and fats are used as fuel by life-forms.

Proteins are more complex. They are the building blocks of a body and are used, for example, to make muscles and skin. Proteins have very large molecules, which include nitrogen, sulfur, and phosphorus atoms as well as carbon, hydrogen, and oxygen atoms. Perhaps the most important organic compound is DNA (deoxyribonucleic acid; *see* p. 58). This molecule forms long chains that carry genes—the coded plans for building a living body.

▲ *A wide range of everyday products that contain organic compounds. They include everything from nylon shirts to CDs and skin lotions.*

occurs when a compound reacts with oxygen. (*see* vol. 3: p. 28). Chemists can calculate the proportions of carbon and hydrogen atoms in an organic compound by measuring the amount of each of these gases produced when it burns.

In 1828 Friedrich Wöhler discovered that organic compounds could be made from inorganic ones (*see* box, p. 5). Chemists began to look at organic compounds in a new way. They looked at simple compounds with just a few atoms in them. These included nut oils, formic acid made by stinging ants, and alcohol made by rotting fruit.

The chemists saw that some compounds react in the same ways even though they are very different in other ways. The scientists realized that these compounds all have the same group of atoms somewhere in their molecule. It is these so-called functional groups that give the compounds their properties. Today's organic chemists study how these functional groups work and even make up new ones.

See Also ...
● *Making Molecules, Vol. 9: pp. 46–65.*

Key Terms

● **Biochemistry:** The study of chemical reactions inside bodies.
● **Inorganic:** Describes a substance that is not organic.
● **Organic:** Describes a compound that is made of carbon and generally also contains hydrogen.

Carbon Bonding

All organic compounds contain carbon atoms. Carbon is the only element with atoms that can form limitless chains as well as branched and ring structures. This ability is a result of the way carbon forms bonds.

Organic compounds exist in a mind-boggling array of shapes and sizes. Their molecules often form chains, rings, and networks of the two, but there are also coiled molecules, spheres, and even tiny tubes (*see* p. 16). All this variety is a result of the ability of carbon atoms to form strong bonds. To understand how carbon atoms form so many molecules, it is worth looking at pure carbon itself.

Diamonds are made from pure carbon. The carbon atoms are connected in a rigid network, which makes diamond the hardest substance known.

PURE FORMS OF CARBON

Carbon occurs in nature in four main forms: soot, fullerenes, diamond, and graphite. Both soot and fullerenes are made when carbon-containing compounds are burned. Fullerenes are very fragile structures and were only discovered 20 years ago (*see* p. 15). Soot, a fine black powder also known as amorphous carbon, does not have an ordered structure; its carbon atoms are arranged randomly.

Graphite and diamond are the two most stable and familiar forms of pure carbon. Despite being made of nothing but carbon atoms, the two substances are very different.

Graphite is a black and shiny material. It glistens in the light slightly, like a metal. Also like a metal, graphite can

A drop of crude petroleum, otherwise known as oil. Oil is a mixture of many carbon-containing compounds, such as tar and gasoline.

conduct electric currents. Graphite is used in pencil leads because it is a very soft substance. When a pencil is moved across a piece of paper, the graphite wears away, leaving a dark line. This dark line is a very thin layer of carbon atoms.

In many ways, diamond is the opposite of graphite. It is see-through and colorless and cannot conduct (carry) electricity. Diamond is also extremely hard, the hardest of all substances, in fact. It is very hard to break a diamond. When diamond crystals do break they split along flat surfaces. This makes it possible to make diamonds into attractive jewels. The points between the surfaces of a diamond are very sharp and hard enough to cut through any solid. Many drills and saws have diamond tips.

CARBON ATOM

How can the atoms of one element make two so very different materials? The answer is in the way the atoms are

Key Terms

- **Amorphous:** Something that has no definite shape.
- **Atom:** The smallest piece of an element that still retains the properties of that element.
- **Element:** A substance made up of just one type of atom.
- **Molecule:** Two or more atoms connected together.
- **Organic:** Describes a compound that is made of carbon and that generally also contains hydrogen.

The carbon atom

Atoms are made up of three types of particles: protons, neutrons, and electrons. Protons and neutrons form the central nucleus. Protons have a positive electric charge; neutrons have no charge. A carbon atom has six protons in its nucleus. Most carbon atoms also have six neutrons, although some rare types have seven or eight.

   Particles called electrons move around the nucleus in two layers, or shells. Electrons are negatively charged and they are attracted to the positive charge of the protons in the nucleus. This force holds the atom together. Carbon atoms have six electrons—the same number as protons. Two electrons move in the inner shell close to the nucleus. The other four reside in the outer shell. An atom's outer electrons are involved in chemical bonds. Carbon atoms can form four bonds with other atoms. This ability is the key to carbon's remarkable chemistry.

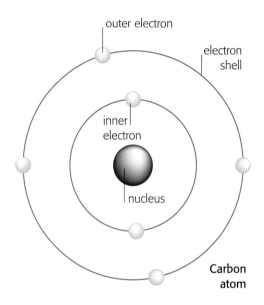

outer electron

electron shell

inner electron

nucleus

Carbon atom

connected inside each substance. To understand how carbon forms bonds, we must look inside an atom of carbon (*see* box above).

   Carbon atoms have four electrons in their outer shell. These electrons are the ones that form bonds with other atoms. Atoms form bonds by sharing, taking, or giving away their outer electrons. They do this to make their outer electron shell full, which makes the atoms stable.

   An atom's outer shell can hold eight electrons. To become stable, a carbon atom must share four electrons with other atoms. A bond formed when atoms share electrons is called a covalent bond. Carbon atoms are unusual, however, because their outer shell is half full (or half empty). That makes the atoms more stable than most. As a result carbon atoms can form two or even three strong bonds with just one other atom (*see* box, p. 11).

▶ *Bubbles of carbon-dioxide (CO_2) gas fizz out of a can. Carbon dioxide and many other carbon compounds are classed as inorganic. However, the carbon atoms in the compounds form bonds in the same way as they do in organic compounds.*

A Closer LOOK

Carbon and covalent bonds

A carbon atom can form up to four covalent bonds. These bonds involve two atoms sharing electrons. In a simple covalent bond, each atom provides one electron, forming a pair. The pair of electrons sits in the outer shell of both atoms. As a result the atoms are pulled side by side. The shared pair of electrons is being pulled on by the positive charge of the nucleus of both atoms. These pulling forces hold, or bond, the atoms together. This arrangement is called a single bond.

A carbon atom can form two or three bonds with one other atom. These are known as double and triple bonds. Most of the time, double and triple bonds form between two carbon atoms.

In a double bond, each atom shares two of its electrons. A triple bond involves three pairs. Compounds with double and triple bonds are more reactive than those with single bonds. The bonds often break so they can form extra more-stable single bonds.

▶ In a single bond, each atom gives one electron, forming a pair shared between both of the atoms. The atoms' other electrons are free to form bonds with other atoms.

▶ In a double bond, each atom gives two electrons, forming two pairs of shared electrons. The bond pulls the two atoms closer together than in a single bond.

▶ In a triple bond each atom gives three electrons, forming three pairs shared between them. The bond pulls the two atoms even closer together.

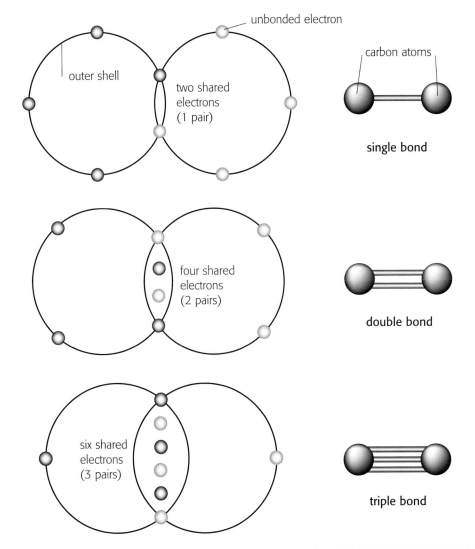

unbonded electron

outer shell

two shared electrons (1 pair)

carbon atoms

single bond

four shared electrons (2 pairs)

double bond

six shared electrons (3 pairs)

triple bond

Carbon's ability to form so-called double and triple bonds is behind the differences between graphite, diamond, and other forms of pure carbon.

DIFFERENT BONDS

Inside a diamond, carbon atoms are connected by only single bonds. Each carbon atom is bonded to the four atoms surrounding it. With all the atoms bonded to one another, a piece of diamond is one huge molecule.

Diamonds are measured in a unit called carats. A one-carat diamond weighs 0.007 ounces (0.2 g). A diamond this size has 10^{23} atoms (the number 10 followed by 23 zeros). In reality, no diamond is perfect, there are always some tiny cracks in the crystal.

▼ *Thick smoke flows out of a large smokestack. Smoke is hot gases that have fine particles of solids mixed into them. Most of the solids are particles of soot. Unlike other forms of carbon, the atoms inside soot are not organized in any ordered patterns.*

Diamond's extreme hardness is a result of its atoms being bonded into a rigid interconnecting structure (*see* box, p. 13). Graphite is so soft and different to diamond in many other ways because some of the atoms inside are joined by a weaker type of bond.

Key Terms

- **Covalent bond:** A bond in which two or more atoms share electrons.
- **Electron shell:** A layer of electrons that surrounds the nucleus of an atom.
- **Inorganic:** Describes a substance that is not organic.
- **Nucleus:** The central core of an atom containing protons and neutrons.

A Closer LOOK

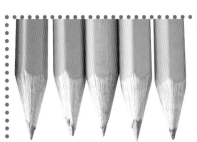

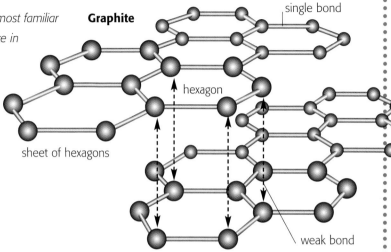

◀ *Graphite is most familiar as the substance in pencil leads.*

Graphite

single bond

hexagon

sheet of hexagons

weak bond

Types of pure carbon

Pure carbon occurs in more than one form. Each form is called an allotrope. The three carbon allotropes are graphite, diamond, and fullerenes. Graphite molecules form as sheets. Each carbon atom is bonded to three others, and they form interconnecting hexagons (six-sided shapes). Each atom also forms a fourth, weaker bond with an atom in a neighboring sheet. As a result, the sheets can move past each other easily, making graphite soft. In diamond, all the bonds are equal in strength. That makes it very difficult to break a diamond apart because there are no weak points in the structure. The last form, fullerenes, are very fragile. They can be described as a single sheet of graphite rolled into a ball.

single bond

Diamond

tetrahedron

▲ In graphite the carbon atoms form sheets of hexagons. Each atom is joined to the sheet above or below by a weak bond. ◀ In diamond, each set of four carbon atoms forms a pyramid-like shape called a tetrahedron. The pyramids are all connected to each another. ▼ This fullerene is a sphere of 60 carbon atoms.

Fullerene (C$_{60}$)

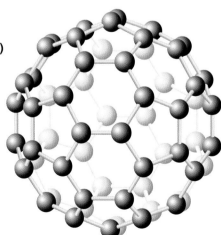

◀ *Diamonds are used as jewels because they reflect light in such a way that they sparkle.*

A Closer LOOK

Other allotropes

Carbon is not the only element to have allotropes—more than one pure form. Pure oxygen, sulfur, tin, and arsenic are some examples of other elements that exist in several forms. Although an element's allotropes look different and have different properties, they are all made up of just one type of atom. However, the arrangement of atoms is different inside each allotrope, and that is what gives each form its different properties.

For example, arsenic exists as gray arsenic and yellow arsenic. The first form is hard and shiny like a piece of metal. However, yellow arsenic is a crumbly powder. Sulfur has several allotropes. Sulfur crystals form many shapes, including spikes and cubes.

Tin is a metal with two allotropes. When it warms up, the element becomes white tin. As it cools down again, it slowly turns back into gray tin. Perhaps the most familiar allotrope is ozone. This is a form of oxygen (*see* box, p. 55).

Inside graphite, each carbon is joined to just three atoms by single bonds. The atom is also connected to a fourth atom, but this time the bond is a weak bond that forms in the same way as a double bond. However, the bond in graphite is not quite the same because only one pair of electrons is shared.

This fourth bond is very weak, and as a result the carbon atoms inside graphite are not as strongly connected to each other. When a force pushes on graphite, it breaks the atoms' weak bonds easily, and the graphite breaks or changes shape. A lump of graphite feels slippery. That is because even the touch of your fingers is enough to rub away a layer of graphite. Graphite is used as a lubricant instead of oil or grease.

▼ Not all carbon-containing compounds are organic. Some simple carbon compounds are classed as inorganic because their carbon atoms do not form chains or rings. These cliffs are made from limestone, which mostly contains calcium carbonate ($CaCO_3$). In this compound, each carbon atom is bonded to three oxygen atoms, and together they are joined to a calcium atom.

Calcium carbonate is a very useful substance. People use it to make chalks, steel, and in construction.

CARRYING ELECTRICITY

The structure of graphite also explains how it carries electricity, though diamond cannot. An electric current is a flow of electrons—sometimes other charged particles—through a substance. The moving particles transfer energy from one place to another, and electric currents are used to power many machines in our homes, schools, and places of work.

Substances that can carry electricity are conductors; they have electrons that are free to move around inside. Insulators—materials that do not carry electricity—do not have free electrons. Graphite is a conductor because the electrons involved in the weak bonds break free easily. They then flow through the graphite crystal between the sheets of carbon atoms. All the electrons in diamond are held in strong bonds and cannot be released to form a current. As a result, diamond is an insulator.

FULLERENES

Fullerenes, the third structural form of carbon, are also conductors. However, the way their electrons are free to move is different again from other carbon allotropes. Looking at the structure of fullerenes will also help us understand the properties of organic compounds.

Fullerenes are made when carbon compounds are burned. These molecules are fragile, and in normal conditions they soon fall apart and form sootlike substances.

The smallest and simplest fullerene contains 60 carbon atoms. Its formula is C_{60}. This fullerene was the first to be

History

Balls from fire

Diamond and graphite have been known about for thousands of years. However, a third form of carbon was discovered only 20 years ago. In 1985, English scientist Harold Kroto (1939–) teamed up with two U.S. chemists Richard Smalley (1943–) and Robert Curl (1933–). The trio were trying to figure out what the surface of a star might be like. They used a superhot laser to burn samples of carbon and then analyzed what was produced.

Their experiments produced a lot of clusters of carbon atoms, like the ones seen in soot. However, to their surprise they found that clusters containing 60 carbon atoms were also produced. These clusters were much bigger than they expected and did not break apart easily. The scientists realized that the carbon atoms must be forming a hollow, cagelike ball. Further experiments showed that balls and other hollow structures could be made with larger numbers of carbon atoms.

Kroto, Smalley, and Curl had discovered a new carbon allotrope and they won the Nobel Prize for chemistry in 1996. They named the substances fullerenes after the U.S. architect R. Buckminster Fuller (1895–1983). In the 1950s, Fuller designed domes that, by chance, had the same shape and structure as the chemicals.

A geodesic dome built by Buckminster Fuller in Montreal, Canada, in 1967.

discovered in 1985. It was named buckminsterfullerene for the designer of geodesic domes, which it resembles (*see* box, p. 15). All similar carbon structures are now referred to as fullerenes, and C_{60} has been nicknamed "the buckyball."

In a buckyball and other fullerenes, each carbon atom is bonded to three others. Most form into hexagons in the same way as in sheets of graphite. However, in a few cases the carbons also form pentagons (five-sided shapes). This sheet of interconnected hexagons and pentagons curves into a sphere.

Unlike in diamond and graphite, the carbon atoms in fullerenes do not form a fourth bond. Instead the spare,

unbonded electrons from each atom are shared between them all. This creates a "cloud" of electrons that spreads evenly over the surface of the ball. The electrons in this cloud are free to move and carry an electric current.

It is hoped that fullerenes will be very useful substances. They have been made into nanotubes (*see* box below). Perhaps

Key Terms

- **Allotrope:** One form of a pure element.
- **Conductor:** A substance that carries electricity and heat well.
- **Crystal:** A solid made of repeating patterns of atoms.
- **Insulator:** A substance that does not transfer an electric current or heat.

Chemistry in Action

Nanotubes

Fullerenes do not have to be balls. In 1991, Japanese scientist Iijima Sumio (1939–) made fullerenes that were tube shaped. The tubes were made from a sheet of carbon atoms bonded in the same hexagon pattern as graphite molecules. The structures were named nanotubes. Nanotubes are very thin. One long enough to stretch from Earth to the Moon could be rolled into a ball the size of a poppy seed! So far, scientists can only make short pieces. If we learn how to make them long enough, there will be many uses for nanotubes. For example, the tubes could be woven to make a material many times stronger than steel but much lighter.

▲ *An illustration of a section of nanotube.*

one day fullerenes will make pipes and wires in tiny machines. Fullerenes are hollow and can hold other atoms inside them. The atom inside is not bonded to the fullerene so the two do not form a compound. Chemists have had to come up with a new way of describing such arrangements. A helium atom (He) inside a buckyball is written as $He@C_{60}$.

ORGANIC COMPOUNDS

The ability of carbon atoms to form different types of bonds is what makes it possible for so many different organic compounds to exist. As you will see, organic compounds include everything from exploding gases to smelly oils to bouncy solids.

▼ Plastic objects are made from long, chainlike organic compounds that can be molded into any shape.

See Also ...
• Reactions and Bonding, Vol. 1: pp. 42–55.
• Carbon, Vol. 7: pp. 10–23.

A Closer LOOK

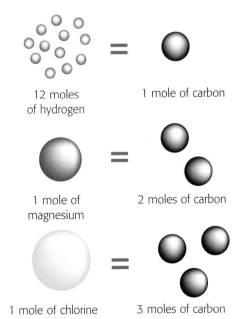

12 moles of hydrogen = 1 mole of carbon

1 mole of magnesium = 2 moles of carbon

1 mole of chlorine = 3 moles of carbon

▲ A diagram showing how the masses of different elements compare with the mass of carbon.

Counting atoms

Atoms are too small to count one by one. How do chemists know how many atoms are contained in something? Chemists count atoms in moles. A mole is very large number. Just as one *dozen* means 12, a *mole* means 602,213,670,000,000,000,000,000. Chemists weigh a substance to calculate how many moles of atoms or molecules it contains.

The atoms of each element have a fixed number of particles in their nucleus. Therefore, the atoms also have a fixed mass. (Electrons are so tiny they do not really affect the atom's mass.) Carbon atoms have 12 times as many particles in their nucleus as hydrogen atoms. Therefore a mole of carbon atoms weighs 12 times as much as a mole of hydrogen atoms. The masses of all atoms can be compared in the same way. Chemists have agreed that carbon will be the benchmark for measuring moles. One mole of carbon weighs 12 grams (0.42 ounces). The mass of a mole of all other elements is based on this measurement.

Carbon Chains

It is the ability of carbon atoms to form into chains that makes organic compounds so varied. There is no limit to the length of these chains, and they might branch into highly complex networks.

The simplest organic compounds contain just carbon (C) and hydrogen (H) atoms. These compounds are called hydrocarbons. Hydrocarbons are very useful substances. They occur mixed together in petroleum oil and natural gas.

Gasoline and other fuels are examples of hydrocarbons. Hydrocarbons are also used to make thousands of other products.

Inside a hydrocarbon molecule, a carbon atom can be bonded to other carbon atoms or it can be connected to

Candle flames are produced when wax melts and burns in the air. The wax is made from a mixture of hydrocarbons called paraffins.

◀ *Traffic runs along busy roads during an evening rush hour. Most automobiles and trucks are fueled with hydrocarbons, such as gasoline and diesel oil.*

hydrogen atoms. Each carbon atom can bond to up to four other atoms. A hydrogen atom, on the other hand, can only form one bond. The hydrogen atoms in hydrocarbon molecules are always bonded to carbon atoms.

STRONG BONDS

Hydrocarbons are covalent compounds. The atoms in their molecules are bonded because they are sharing electrons.

Carbon atoms can form into long chains because the bond between two carbon atoms is very stable. That is because carbon atoms have an outer electron shell that is half full (*see* p. 10).

The bond between a hydrogen and a carbon atom is also a strong one. Hydrogen atoms form stable bonds for the same reason that carbon atoms do.

Hydrogen atoms have one electron shell. This shell can hold only two electrons, and hydrogen atoms have one. As a result, their electron shell is half full, just like in a carbon atom.

Key Terms

- **Compound:** A substance formed when atoms of two or more different elements bond together.
- **Covalent bond:** A bond that forms between two or more atoms when they share electrons.
- **Hydrocarbon:** A type of organic compound containing only carbon and hydrogen atoms.
- **Molecule:** Two or more atoms connected together.

Hydrogen atoms can only form one bond each, so they cannot form chains. However, hydrogen forms the most complex and varied set of compounds in chemistry, when bonded with carbon.

ALKANES

The simplest hydrocarbon compounds are made of atoms connected by single bonds. This group of hydrocarbons is called the alkanes. Being made up of single bonds, alkane molecules have the same pyramid structure of diamond (*see* p. 13). However, the atoms form chains instead of a rigid network as in diamond. The shapes of alkanes and other organic compounds are complex, so all molecules are shown here as flat diagrams.

The smallest alkane is methane. This has the formula CH_4. A carbon atom is bonded to four hydrogen atoms. The next alkane is called ethane (C_2H_6). It has two carbon atoms bonded together. Each

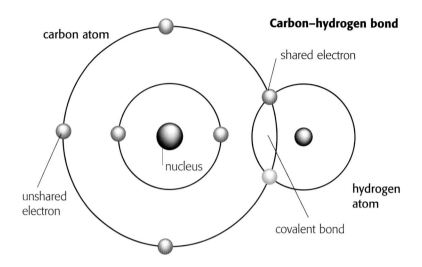

Carbon–hydrogen bond

carbon atom; shared electron; nucleus; unshared electron; hydrogen atom; covalent bond

▲ *The covalent bond between a carbon and hydrogen atom.*

carbon atom is attached to three hydrogen atoms. The next compound, propane (C_3H_8), has three carbons in a row, while butane (C_4H_{10}) has four.

Alkane molecules get larger by adding more carbon atoms. The compounds have the general formula $C_nH_{(2n+2)}$, where n is the number of carbon atoms in a molecule. For example, in methane n equals 1, so the number of hydrogen atoms is $(2 \times 1) + 2 = 4$.

NAMING SYSTEM

With so many compounds to understand, chemists have developed a system for naming organic compounds. They have

▼ *Hydrocarbons are not just found on Earth. A recent probe to Titan, a moon of the planet Saturn, found clouds and pools of methane on the moon. This is the probe's view as imagined by an artist.*

Names of molecules

Number of carbon atoms	Prefix
1	Meth-
2	Eth-
3	Prop-
4	But-
5	Pent-
6	Hex-
7	Hept-
8	Oct-
9	Non-
10	Dec-

agreed on a prefix (the beginning of a word) for each number of carbon atoms in a molecule. For example, the prefix for two atoms is *eth-*, while molecules with eight atoms begin with *oct-* (*see* box, p. 20). All alkane compounds end in *-ane*. Therefore, C_2H_6 is called ethane and C_8H_{18} is named octane. The same system is used for other groups of hydrocarbons.

ALKANE CHEMISTRY

As we have learned, the bonds in alkane molecules are very stable. As a result, alkane compounds are not very reactive. Their most important reaction is combustion, or burning. Combustion reactions occur when compounds react with oxygen (O; *see* vol. 3: p. 28).

When alkanes burn they release a lot of energy. That is why they make good fuels. For example, the natural gas extracted from underground is mainly methane. This gas is used in cooktops, ovens, and boilers, and is also burned in power plants to make electricity.

The combustion reaction also produces carbon dioxide (CO_2) and water (H_2O). All hydrocarbons produce these compounds when they burn, but

Key Terms

- **Alkane:** A hydrocarbon chain in which all atoms are connected by single bonds.
- **Chemical equation:** Symbols and numbers that show how reactants change into products during a reaction.
- **Combustion:** The reaction that causes burning. Combustion is generally a reaction with oxygen in the air.

A Closer LOOK

The alkanes

Alkane molecules are made using only single bonds. All carbon atoms in the molecules are bonded to the maximum of four other atoms. Many of the most familiar hydrocarbons are alkanes. Gasoline fuel contains a lot of octane (C_8H_{18}). Paraffin wax used to make candles is a mixture of alkane compounds each containing between 22 and 27 carbon atoms.

▼ The three simplest alkanes.

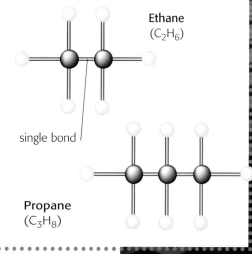

Methane (CH_4)

hydrogen atom

carbon atom

Ethane (C_2H_6)

single bond

Propane (C_3H_8)

▶ Flames burn on a barbecue. The fuels being burned are methane and propane.

Chemistry in Action

Heating Earth

Gasoline and other fuels are often called "fossil fuels." That is because the petroleum oil, natural gas, and coal located deep beneath the ground are the remains of plants and other life-forms that died millions of the years ago. Over the years, their remains have been buried, then heated and squeezed under the ground until they broke down into hydrocarbons. The carbon these compounds contain was taken from the air when the life-forms were alive. They used it to build their bodies.

For millions of years, that carbon has been locked underground. People today bring fossil fuels to the surface and burn them as fuels. When the hydrocarbons burn they react with oxygen and produce carbon dioxide and water (*see* p. 21). These products are released into the air.

People have been burning fossil fuels for about 200 years. In that time, the amount of carbon dioxide in Earth's atmosphere has increased by 50 percent. Earth's atmosphere acts like a blanket around the planet. It traps heat and keeps the world warm. However, now that the atmosphere has more carbon dioxide, it seems to be trapping too much heat.

The world is warming up because of all the carbon dioxide we are releasing as we burn fuels. Experts think that in 100 years, Earth will be about 5 degrees Fahrenheit (5°F; 3°C) warmer. That is likely to cause huge changes to the world's weather.

▲ *Nobody knows what a warmer world will be like. Some places will dry out into deserts, and other areas will be flooded by the sea.*

Oil and fats, such as those in butter, belong to a group of hydrocarbons called lipids. Oils are unsaturated lipids, while fats are saturated lipids.

the two carbon atoms are connected by a double bond (*see* p. 11). With two bonds used up connecting to the other atom, some of the carbon atoms have just two bonds left for hydrogen atoms.

The alkenes increase in size in the same way as the alkanes: propene (C_3H_6) contains three carbon atoms, butene (C_4H_8) contains four, and so on. As with the alkanes, there is no limit to the length of an alkene chain.

ALKENE CHEMISTRY

Alkenes occur in petroleum mixed in with alkanes and other hydrocarbons. However, people also make alkenes because the double bonds make alkenes useful. Whereas alkanes are just burned as fuel, alkenes can be reacted with other compounds to make many products.

different hydrocarbons produce them in different amounts. The equation for the combustion of methane is:

$$CH_4 + 2O_2 \rightarrow CO_2 + 2H_2O$$

ALKENES

In an alkane, each carbon atom has four single bonds. Chemists say that alkanes are saturated hydrocarbons: the atoms inside are all bonded to the maximum number of other atoms. A molecule that contains carbon atoms that are bonded to less than four other atoms is described as being unsaturated.

Hydrocarbons that contain carbon atoms bonded to just three other atoms are called alkenes. The simplest alkene is ethene (C_2H_4). In a molecule of ethene,

A Closer LOOK

The alkenes

A hydrocarbon containing carbon atoms that are joined by double bonds is called an alkene. The double bonds fix the shape of an alkene molecule. Single bonds allow sections of the molecule to spin around independently. The double bond cannot rotate so sections of the molecule cannot move. This has most effect on the structures of branched molecules (*see* box, p. 25), where branches are attached on certain sides of the double bond.

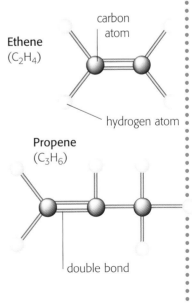

Ethene (C_2H_4)

carbon atom

hydrogen atom

Propene (C_3H_6)

double bond

The two simplest alkenes.

Alkenes are reactive because a double bond readily breaks to form two single bonds. For example, alkenes will react with hydrogen gas (H_2) to become alkanes. The reaction that turns ethene into ethane has the following equation:

$$C_2H_4 + H_2 \rightarrow C_2H_6$$

This reaction is called an addition reaction because hydrogen has been added to the molecule.

ALKYNES

Hydrocarbons that contain triple bonds between two carbon atoms (*see* p. 11) are called alkynes. This group of compounds is more reactive than the alkenes. That is because a triple bond breaks to form three single bonds even more easily than a double bond does. Alkynes are so reactive they are not very common in petroleum oil. Instead people make alkynes. The simplest alkyne is ethyne (C_2H_2), also called acetylene.

▶ *An oxyacetylene torch used to cut through solid steel. The extremely hot flame is produced by burning acetylene, also known as ethyne.*

A Closer LOOK

The alkynes

Alkynes are hydrocarbons that have carbon atoms connected to each other by triple bonds. The simplest alkyne is ethyne. In this molecule each carbon is bonded to just one hydrogen. Larger alkyne molecules do not have triple bonds between all the carbon atoms. Just one triple bond is enough to make them alkynes.

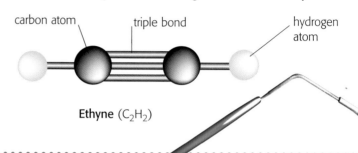

carbon atom   triple bond   hydrogen atom

Ethyne (C_2H_2)

Key Terms

- **Alkene:** A hydrocarbon chain in which at least two carbon atoms are connected by a double bond.
- **Alkyne:** A hydrocarbon chain in which at least two carbon atoms are connected by a triple bond.
- **Saturated:** A hydrocarbon molecule in which all the carbon atoms are bonded to four other atoms. An unsaturated molecule contains double or triple bonds between carbon atoms.

Like the alkenes, alkynes are used to make useful chemicals, such as plastics and medicines. However, ethyne is also used in torches for welding and cutting metal. It burns with oxygen at up to 6,300 degrees Fahrenheit (6,300°F; 3,500°C)—much hotter than other fuels.

PETROCHEMICALS

Before hydrocarbons such as alkanes and alkenes can be used for fuels or in industry, they must be refined. Refined hydrocarbons are called petrochemicals.

The main source of hydrocarbons is petroleum. This is a mixture of gases, liquids, and sludgelike solids. The word *petroleum* comes from the two Latin words for "rock" and "oil." Most petroleum is deep underground and it must be pumped to the surface. Petroleum is the remains of life-forms that have become buried under rocks over millions of years (*see* box, p. 22).

▼ *A refinery where petrochemicals are produced.*

Branched molecules

Not all hydrocarbons are straight chains. Molecules with four or more carbon atoms can divide into branches. A branched molecule may contain the same number of atoms as a straight molecule, and their chemical formulas will be the same. Chemists use the naming system to describe how each molecule is organized instead.

A molecule's name is determined by the size of its longest straight chain. Alkane 1 (below) has four carbon atoms in a single chain. It is therefore named butane.

Alkane 1

butane
(C_4H_{10})

Alkane 2 also has four carbon atoms. However, its longest chain has three carbon atoms (like propane). The other carbon and its three hydrogen atoms ($-CH_3$, or methyl) are attached to the middle of the chain. The molecule is named methyl propane.

Alkane 2

methyl propane

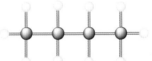

methyl group ($-CH_3$)

Alkane 3 has two methyls each attached to different carbon atoms. Numbers are added to the name to show where the methyls join the chain: 2,3 dimethylbutane.

Alkane 3

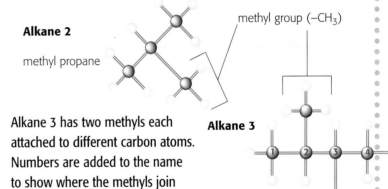

2,3-dimethylbutane

Methyls and other branches are called alkyl groups. Their names are based on the number of carbon atoms they contain:

Number of carbons	Alkyl group	Formula
1	Methyl-	$-CH_3$
2	Ethyl-	$-C_2H_5$
3	Propyl-	$-C_3H_7$
4	Butyl-	$-C_4H_9$

FRACTIONS

Unrefined petroleum is called crude oil. Once at a refinery, any gases, water, and unwanted solids, such as mud, are removed. The hydrocarbons that remain are then pumped into the bottom of a tall tower and heated to 720°F (380°C).

The tower is a fractional distillation column. It is used to separate the different sizes, or fractions, of hydrocarbon molecules. Heating the petroleum makes most of the hydrocarbons boil and turn into a gas (*see* vol. 2: p. 62).

The mixture of gases flows up the column. As the gas rises, it begins to cool down and turn into liquids. These liquids are collected at several points inside the column. Small and light hydrocarbon molecules, such as pentane

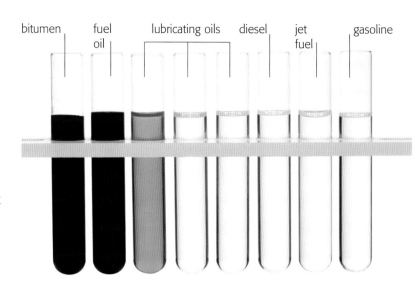

bitumen | fuel oil | lubricating oils | diesel | jet fuel | gasoline

▲ *Fractions refined from crude oil. Bitumen has the highest boiling point. Gasoline has the lowest.*

(C_5H_{12}), have lower boiling points than large and heavy ones. The light molecules stay as gases until they get to the top of the column, where they are collected. Heavier fractions turn to liquid at points lower down, where they are collected.

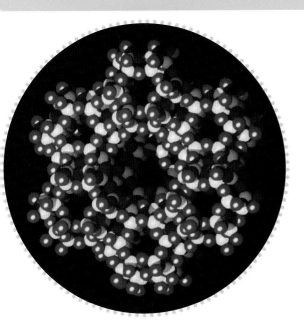

△ *A computer graphic of a zeolite crystal used as a catalyst for making petrochemicals. This particular shape of crystal is used to "crack" long alkanes into smaller, branched molecules.*

BREAKING THE CHAINS

Most of the hydrocarbons in crude oil are alkanes with straight chains. Around 90 percent of crude oil ends up as fuel—mainly gasoline for cars. However, after the fractions have been separated, only about 20 percent of them are useful immediately. The rest are pumped into chambers called reactors, where they are converted into more useful molecules.

Inside the reactors, the hydrocarbons are "cracked." Cracking is a process that breaks long alkane molecules into shorter alkanes and alkenes. Cracking requires the hydrocarbons to be very hot and under high pressure, but that alone is not enough. Cracking reactions require catalysts. A catalyst is a substance that helps a reaction along but is not changed after the reaction has finished.

◁ *A fractional distillation column at a refinery.*

A Closer LOOK

A catalyst at work

Some chemical reactions occur only very slowly or require very high temperatures. A catalyst is a substance that makes a reaction run more quickly and so saves time and money. It works by bringing the reactants (the reaction's ingredients) together so they can rearrange into the products. However, a catalyst is not used up by the reaction, so it can keep on working with new reactants.

Catalysts are also used to make sure that the correct reactions occur instead of other unwanted ones. Solid catalysts are used so they do not get mixed up with gas or liquid reactants. For example, a solid cobalt catalyst is used to react methane with oxygen to make larger alkane molecules, such as ethane:

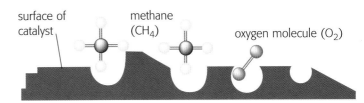

surface of catalyst   methane (CH_4)   oxygen molecule (O_2)

△ *The molecules are brought together on the surface of the catalyst.*

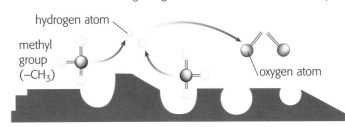

hydrogen atom

methyl group (−CH_3)

oxygen atom

△ *The oxygen molecule splits into single atoms. One oxygen atom pulls a hydrogen from each methane molecule, turning them into methyl groups.*

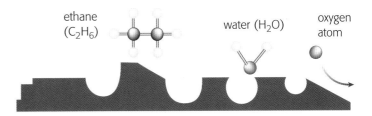

ethane (C_2H_6)   water (H_2O)   oxygen atom

△ *The two methyl groups bond together to form a molecule of ethane. The hydrogen atoms bond to the oxygen to make water. The second oxygen atom reacts with other methane molecules.*

The catalysts used in cracking are zeolites. These are very complex hollow structures made from aluminum and silicon compounds. The hydrocarbons crack into smaller molecules as they are pumped through the zeolites.

GOOD GASOLINE

The cracked hydrocarbons are then separated into fractions in the same way as before. Again only some of the products are useful as fuel. However, this time the unwanted molecules are too small and light to be used in gasoline.

The best hydrocarbons for gasoline are small, branched alkanes. They burn more slowly than unbranched compounds and keep an engine running smoothly.

▼ Oil wells are often in remote places. The crude oil is pumped through long pipes to refineries or to ports, where it is loaded onto a ship called a tanker, which then delivers the oil to a refinery.

A Closer LOOK

Almost organic

▲ Windshields of cars and other vehicles are coated with a thin layer of chain molecules of silicon atoms called silanes. The silanes stop rainwater from clinging to the glass so the driver can see out better.

Carbon and hydrogen can form into any size of molecule. However, a couple of other elements—silicon and boron—can also form chains, too, only much shorter. Silicon and boron share certain properties with carbon. Silicon (Si) has four electrons in its outer shell, just like carbon. However, it has larger atoms, and they bond weakly with hydrogen. Nevertheless hydrogen and silicon atoms can form short chains that are similar to alkanes. These compounds are called silanes. Only monosilane (SiH_4) is very stable on its own. Boron (B) atoms are slightly smaller than carbon's. They have three outer electrons and can form only three bonds at once. Chains made from boron and hydrogen atoms are called boranes. The simplest is diborane (B_2H_6).

562

◄ *A miner digs out coal in a mine deep underground. Coal is mainly pure carbon, but that can be converted into useful hydrocarbons using catalysts such as cobalt and nickel.*

See ALSO ...
● *Catalysts,*
Vol. 4: pp. 56–65.
● *Chemistry in Industry,*
Vol. 10: pp. 4–21.

Another process, called alkylation, converts the small, light alkanes and alkenes produced by cracking into larger branched alkanes. The catalysts used in alkylation are strong acids.

COAL

Crude oil is not the only source of hydrocarbons. Coal is a rock made from pure carbon mixed with hydrocarbons. Coal is used as a fuel and is reacted with ores to make pure metals (*see* vol. 6: box p. 53). In the past coal was a source of a fuel called coal gas. This gas is poisonous and has been replaced with natural gas. However, coal may become a useful source of petrochemicals in the future.

Chemistry in Action

Oil spills

Every day the world uses 85 million barrels of oil. One barrel of oil contains 42 gallons (159 liters). That adds up to 150 million gallons an hour! All this oil needs to reach refineries. Most of the oil is taken in giant ships called tankers.

The largest tankers carry 400,000 tons (360 metric tons) of oil. What happens when a tanker spills its oil? Crude oil floats on water forming a "slick." Sometimes the gasoline and other fuels catch fire. If the slick can be kept together out at sea with long booms, it can be cleared up. Oil that washes onto the coast and into the mouths of rivers will kill fish, birds, and other wildlife and takes months to clear away.

▲ *An oil slick in a river mouth in the United Kingdom caused when a tanker hit nearby rocks in 1996. The slick took a year to clean up.*

Carbon Rings

As well as chains, hydrocarbon compounds can also form rings. Many of these ringed molecules have unusual properties.

Hydrocarbon molecules that form chains follow a structure that is similar to that of diamond (*see* p. 13). Like in a diamond crystal, the carbon and hydrogen atoms form into a series of pyramid structures. However, there are hydrocarbons with structures that are more similar to graphite.

Like diamond, graphite is a form of pure carbon. Instead of forming pyramids, the atoms in graphite form hexagons, or six-sided rings. Hydrocarbon molecules that contain similar hexagons are called arenes. Another name for them is aromatic compounds, because many of them have a strong aroma (odor).

Pieces of styrofoam are made from a plastic called polystyrene that has been pumped full of air. Polystyrene is made up of many ringed molecules joined together.

Key Terms

- **Atom:** The smallest piece of an element that still retains the properties of that element.
- **Compound:** A substance formed when atoms of two or more different elements bond together.
- **Hydrocarbon:** A type of organic compound containing only carbon (C) and hydrogen (H) atoms.
- **Molecule:** Two or more atoms connected by chemical bonds.

BENZENE

The simplest arene is a compound called benzene. A benzene molecule contains six carbon (C) atoms and six hydrogen (H) atoms. The compound's chemical formula is C_6H_6.

The six carbon atoms are connected into a hexagon. Each carbon atom is also bonded to a single hydrogen atom. Carbon atoms form a total of four bonds. In benzene the carbon atoms are connected to just three other atoms. Thus, each carbon atom forms a double bond (*see* p. 11) with one of its neighboring carbon atoms. As a result, the hexagon of atoms is held together with a mixture of single and double bonds. The two types of bond are arranged alternately (*see* box below).

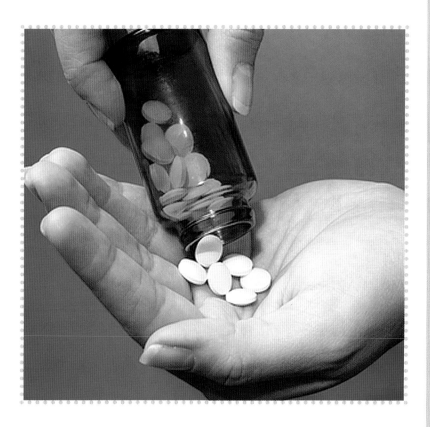

A Closer LOOK

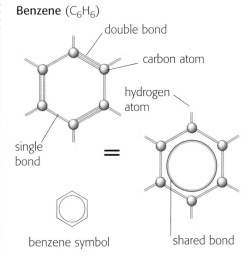

Benzene (C_6H_6)

double bond

carbon atom

hydrogen atom

single bond

=

benzene symbol

shared bond

The benzene ring

Benzene (C_6H_6) is the simplest arene. Its six carbon atoms form a ring. They are connected to each other by three single and three double bonds. The position of these bonds is not fixed. The double bonds and single bonds can swap places. As a result the molecule's three double bonds become shared between all six carbon atoms.

◀ *Two ways of showing the structure of benzene.*

⬛ *Aspirin, one of the most commonly used painkillers, is a compound called acetylsalicylic acid. This compound is an arene. It has molecules containing a ring of six carbon atoms.*

SHARING ELECTRONS

The bonds in a molecule of benzene are covalent (*see* vol. 1: box p. 49). A covalent bond forms between atoms that are sharing electrons. The single bonds in the benzene molecule form when two carbon atoms share a pair of electrons (*see* p. 11). The double bonds form when two atoms share two pairs of electrons.

The two pairs of electrons in a double bond are not the same. The first pair forms in the same way as a pair in a single bond. The second pair of electrons are held together less strongly. They are more likely to break apart and form a bond with another atom.

▶ *Three carbon atoms are connected by a single and double bond.*

▶ *The positions of the single and double bond can swap sides.*

▶ *The second pair of electrons from the double bond becomes delocalized and shared by all the atoms.*

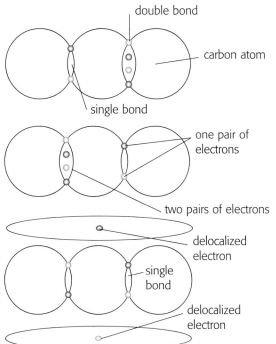

double bond

carbon atom

single bond

one pair of electrons

two pairs of electrons

delocalized electron

single bond

delocalized electron

A Closer LOOK

Arene compounds

An arene is any compound that contains one or more benzene-like rings in its molecule. Arene compounds may have a chain of carbon atoms (an alkyl group; *see* box, p. 25) branching out from the ring in place of a hydrogen atom. Other arene molecules contain two or more joined rings.

▶ *Some simple arenes.*

Naphthalene
$C_{10}H_8$

$-CH_3$ (methyl)

Xylene
$C_6H_4(CH_3)_2$

xylene symbol

Toluene
$C_6H_4CH_3$

naphthalene symbol

toluene symbol

In a benzene ring each of the carbon atoms has formed a single and a double bond with the two carbon atoms on either side. Because the carbon atoms are connected in a ring, they all form a single bond on one side, and a double bond on the other. For example, if one atom has a single bond on its left side and a double on the right, then all the other carbon atoms in the molecule will have those bonds in the same positions.

However, one pair of electrons can move from one side of the carbon atom to the other. As it does this, the double bond becomes a single bond, while the single bond becomes a double. As a result, that pair of electrons is effectively shared between the bonds on both sides of the atom. Because the carbon atoms form a ring, their double bonds fuse into a single shared bond.

▶ *Certain nylons, such those in this rope, are made from ringed hydrocarbons that are not arenes.*

◀ *A diagram showing how the electrons in the double bonds in a benzene molecule become delocalized and shared between all the atoms.*

The electrons inside this shared bond are described as delocalized. They are not linked to one bond but shared between the bonds connecting several atoms. In benzene, the six delocalized electrons move around in doughnut-shaped spaces above and below the ring of carbon atoms.

STABLE MOLECULES

All arene compounds contain rings held together with delocalized electrons. Some arene compounds have a single ring with chained sections attached to them. Other arenes are made up of several rings joined together.

A Closer LOOK

Other rings

Some ringed hydrocarbon molecules are not aromatic. The carbon atoms in these compounds may be connected by single bonds or have just one double bond. There are no delocalized electrons as in benzene molecules. Ringed compounds like this are called alicyclic compounds. Their chemical behavior is similar to that of alkanes or alkenes (*see* pp. 21–24).

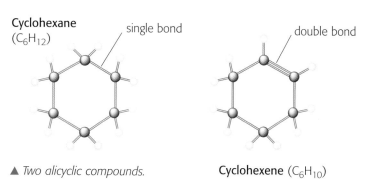

Cyclohexane (C_6H_{12})   single bond   double bond

▲ *Two alicyclic compounds.*   Cyclohexene (C_6H_{10})

Key Terms

- **Arene:** A type of hydrocarbon compound that has ringed molecules.
- **Aromatic:** Describes a compound that contains one or more benzene rings.
- **Benzene:** The simplest arene.
- **Covalent bond:** A bond in which two or more atoms share electrons.
- **Electron:** A tiny particle located inside an atom. Electrons are involved in forming bonds between atoms.

Chemistry in Action

Making a bang

One of the most familiar and common explosives is an arene compound. Most people have heard of TNT. These letters stand for trinitrotoluene. TNT is used in bombs, to demolish old buildings, and to blast away rocks in mines.

Toluene is an arene compound. It is a benzene ring with a methyl group ($-CH_3$) attached. A molecule of TNT is a toluene molecule that also has three nitro groups ($-NO_2$) attached.

When it explodes, TNT is very powerful. However, it is also relatively stable. It does not react easily and stays safe when it gets hot or wet. TNT will explode if a detonator is used to make it hot enough to react; that is 563 degrees Fahrenheit (563°F; 295°C). At this temperature the molecules of TNT break apart, and the nitro groups react with each other to make gases. These gases expand very rapidly and cause a shockwave in the air. It is this shockwave that causes damage to solid objects in its path.

The power of large explosions is measured in kilotons. A 1-kiloton explosion releases the same amount of energy as an explosion of 1,000 tons of TNT.

▶ *A bridge is knocked down, or demolished, using several explosions of TNT. Small amounts of TNT have been positioned on the bridge and exploded all at once. The explosions break the bridge into small pieces, which fall safely into the water.*

The delocalized electrons make the molecules of benzene and other arenes more stable than many other hydrocarbons. Chemists measure how strongly the atoms in a molecule are bonded to each other by measuring how much heat is released when the compound burns (*see* vol. 4: pp. 18–29).

Burning is a reaction between a compound and oxygen (O_2). During the reaction, the compound breaks apart and its atoms bond with oxygen atoms (*see* vol. 3: p. 28). The heat released during burning is the energy left over after the old molecules have broken apart and formed into new ones. More stable hydrocarbons release less heat when they burn. That is because more of the energy has been used up breaking the strong bonds in their molecules.

Chemists can measure how strong a single bond between two carbon atoms is by burning simple alkanes (*see* p. 20). They can also test the strength of a double bond by burning an alkene (*see* p. 23). Chemists could then add these values together to figure out how strong the three single and three double bonds are in a ring of benzene.

However, when this result is tested by burning benzene in a laboratory, chemists find that the molecule's bonds are stronger than they thought. The delocalized electrons are shared equally among all the bonds, making them all stronger.

ARENE CHEMISTRY

The stability of the delocalized electrons has an effect on the way benzene and other arenes react. Hydrocarbons with

Profile

Discovering benzene

Michael Faraday is one of the most important scientists in history. He discovered many things about electricity and magnetism. With that understanding, he invented the first electricity generator and the first electric motor. However, one of Faraday's first discoveries is less well known. For it was Faraday who discovered benzene.

Michael Faraday was born close to London, England, in 1791. The young Michael often went hungry and was not able to get a good education. Nevertheless, at the age of 14 Faraday was already experimenting, using home-made batteries to investigate electricity.

At the age of 20, Faraday became the apprentice (assistant) of Humphry Davy (1778–1829). At that time, Davy was making many discoveries. He had used electricity to purify several then-unknown elements, including the metals sodium and potassium.

Faraday completed his service with Davy in 1820. At first he studied chemistry, only turning to physics ten years later. In 1820, Faraday produced the first chlorocarbons (compounds of chlorine and carbon; *see* p. 54). In 1825 he described a liquid compound, which he named bicarbuet of hydrogen. A few years later, the German chemist Eilhard Mitscherlich (1794–1863) renamed this compound *benzene* after making it from benzoin resin.

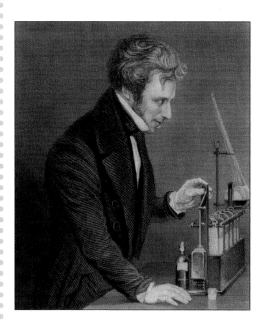

◄ *Faraday at work in his laboratory in the 1840s, a few years after he had discovered benzene.*

double bonds in their molecules tend to be reactive. That is because the double bond easily breaks open and forms two single bonds. For example, an alkene will react with hydrogen (H_2) to become an alkane (*see* p. 24). In this reaction the alkene's double bond breaks and forms single bonds with hydrogen atoms.

That sort of reaction is called an addition, because the hydrogen atoms are *added* to the molecule. With three double bonds in its molecule, you might expect benzene also to be reactive in that

▶ *A liquid pesticide is sprayed onto a field to kill insects that attack crop plants. Many pesticides contain arene compounds.*

Chemistry in Action

▲ *Textile workers mix dyes. About half of the dyes used today are arene compounds called azo dyes.*

Azo dyes

Many of the dyes used to color our clothes are aromatic compounds. These compounds are called azo dyes because they contain a section in the molecule called an azo group. An azo group is formed when one part of a hydrocarbon is connected to another section by two nitrogen (N) atoms. The nitrogen atoms sit between the two parts of the molecule and are connected to each other by a double bond.

Azo groups can form in chained hydrocarbons, but these compounds are very unstable. However, when an azo group attaches to a benzene ring, it forms a stable molecule. The double bond between the nitrogen atoms becomes part of the benzene's system of delocalized electrons. That keeps the molecule stable.

Many azo compounds are brightly colored, mostly red, orange, or yellow. Azo dyes were first used in the 1880s. The first was called Congo red. However, this and other early dyes have been replaced with other azo dyes, which last longer. Most azo dyes are poisonous, but some, such as tartrazine yellow, are used to color food.

Chemistry in Action

See ALSO ...
• *Understanding Electrons, Vol. 1: pp. 36–41.*

Mothballs

Have you heard the expression "put into mothballs?" People say it to mean something is being stored for a long time. The expression comes from the way people sometimes add mothballs to clothes before packing them away for a long time. The small balls are made from naphthalene, an arene compound. The smell of the balls keeps moths away. Moth caterpillars would otherwise eat the wool and cotton in the clothes and make holes in them.

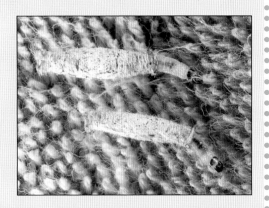

▲ *The caterpillars of clothes moths eat natural fibers and also make a body case out of them.*

▼ *A chemist holds a solution of fullerene dissolved in benzene. Fullerenes are a type of pure carbon found in soot. Like benzene and other arenes, fullerenes have delocalized electrons.*

way. However, benzene and other arenes do not take part in addition reactions with hydrogen. The delocalized electrons stop the molecule's double bonds from breaking and forming into single bonds.

Instead, arenes undergo displacement reactions, where an atom or molecule takes the place of one of the hydrogen atoms. Only very reactive elements, such as the halogens (*see* vol. 7: pp. 48–59), will react with arenes in this way. For example, chlorine (Cl_2) reacts with benzene (C_6H_6) to make chlorobenzene (C_6H_5Cl) and hydrochloric acid (HCl). The chemical equation for this reaction is:

$$C_6H_6 + Cl_2 \rightarrow C_6H_5Cl + HCl$$

POISONS AND CURES

Benzene and several other arene compounds are very poisonous. Even a tiny amount of benzene in food or water

is enough to make a person ill. Benzene damages the body's immune system and nerves and causes cancer. Many pesticides (compounds used to kill pests) are arenes. However, many life-saving medicines and painkillers are also arene compounds.

Alcohols and Acids

Not all organic compounds are hydrocarbons. Many of them contain atoms of other elements. Oxygen is a common ingredient in organic compounds. These compounds include alcohols and organic acids, such as vinegar.

Glasses of red and white white. Wine is an alcoholic beverage made from grape juice. The sugar in the juice reacts with oxygen to make alcohol.

Hydrocarbons are compounds that contain just carbon (C) and hydrogen (H) atoms. As we have seen, the bonds between atoms of these elements are very strong and unlikely to break. As a result, hydrocarbons are not very reactive. However, when atoms of other elements are added to the compounds, they become more reactive. That is because the bonds between the

A Closer LOOK

Alcohols

When a hydroxyl group (–OH) containing an oxygen and hydrogen atom joins to a hydrocarbon chain, it forms a compound called an alcohol. Alcohols are named according to the number of carbons in their molecules (*see* box, p. 20). Their names generally end in –*ol.*

▶ *Three simple alcohol compounds.*

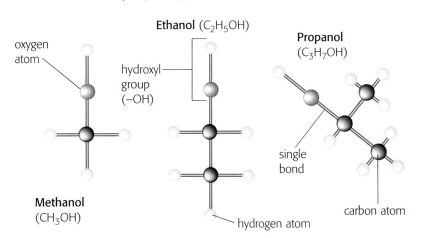

Ethanol (C_2H_5OH)

oxygen atom

hydroxyl group (–OH)

Propanol (C_3H_7OH)

single bond

Methanol (CH_3OH)

hydrogen atom

carbon atom

---

carbon atoms and these other atoms are much weaker and more likely to break open and take part in a reaction.

The section of an organic molecule that contains an atom that is not carbon or hydrogen is called a functional group. The structure of a functional group determines how that compound will react with other chemicals.

ADDING OXYGEN

Oxygen (O) forms a number of functional groups in organic compounds. An oxygen atom can form a total of two bonds with other atoms. For example, water is a compound of oxygen and hydrogen. One oxygen atom is bonded to two hydrogen atoms to make the molecule H_2O. Imagine if one of the hydrogen atoms was replaced with a carbon atom in a

hydrocarbon molecule. That hydrocarbon would then have an oxygen and hydrogen (–OH) attached to it. This –OH structure is a functional group called a hydroxyl. Organic chain compounds with a hydroxyl group belong to the group of compounds called the alcohols (*see* box above).

Key Terms

- **Compound:** A substance formed when atoms of two or more different elements bond.
- **Hydrocarbon:** An organic compound containing only carbon and hydrogen atoms.
- **Functional group:** A part of an organic molecule that

gives it certain chemical properties.
- **Molecule:** Two or more atoms connected together.
- **Organic:** Describes a compound that contains carbon and generally hydrogen but also atoms of other elements.

Hydroxyl groups on an arene compound (*see* pp. 30–37) form compounds called phenols (*see* box, p. 42).

MAKING ALCOHOLS

Alcohols are some of the most familiar organic compounds. They occur naturally, and people have been making them for thousands of years. The most common alcohol compound is ethanol (C_2H_5OH). Ethanol is often called grain alcohol because it can be made from sugars in grain and fruits. That occurs through a series of reactions called fermentation.

Fermentation reactions involve sugar reacting with oxygen. They occur in nature, and they are used to make alcoholic beverages (*see* box below.)

The other common type of alcohol is methanol (CH_3OH). This compound is sometimes called wood alcohol because it can be made by heating wood. If the wood is kept out of the air so it does not burn, it will produce methanol vapors.

Methanol is poisonous, just like all alcohols. Only ethanol can be consumed in small quantities. But in large amounts even ethanol can kill. Most of the simple alcohols are used as solvents (*see* vol. 2: pp. 34–45).

(*see* vol. 2: pp. 34–45).

Key Terms

- **Electron:** A tiny particle that makes up part of an atom. Electrons have a negative charge.
- **Fermentation:** A reaction in which sugar is turned into ethanol.
- **Hydroxyl:** A functional group made up of an oxygen and a hydrogen atom.

Chemistry in Action

Fermentation

Alcoholic drinks, such as wine and beer, are made using a natural process called fermentation. Ethanol (C_2H_5OH) is produced by fermenting glucose, a sugar ($C_6H_{12}O_6$). The reaction also produces carbon dioxide (CO_2). Fermentation occurs inside living cells. The reaction releases energy. The equation for the reaction is:

$$C_6H_{12}O_6 \rightarrow 2C_2H_5OH + 2CO_2$$

The alcohol in wine and beer is fermented by yeast cells. For wine, the sugar comes from grapes. For beer, it comes from grains. The yeast turns the sugars into ethanol until the amount of alcohol gets so high it kills the yeast. As a result, drinks made like this are not more than about 12 percent ethanol. Strongly alcoholic drinks, such as whiskey, are made by purifying the ethanol.

◀ *Beer is made by fermenting grains and hops.*

A Closer LOOK

Isomers

Alcohol compounds with three or more carbon atoms form isomers. Isomers are molecules that contain the same atoms, but those atoms are arranged in different ways. Isomers have the same formula but their molecules have a different shape. Those shapes may create different functional groups and so effect the molecule's behavior.

For example, there are three isomers with the formula C_3H_8O. Two of them are types of propanol (C_3H_7OH), because they each have a hydroxl group (–OH). The two molecules are called propan-1-ol and propan-2-ol (rubbing alcohol). The number tells us which carbon atom has the hydroxyl group attached.

The third isomer is not an alcohol. Instead of forming a hydroxyl group, the oxygen atom joins two carbon atoms together. A molecule with this functional group is called an ether (*see* p. 47). This ether is called methoxyethane. Ethers react in different ways to alcohols.

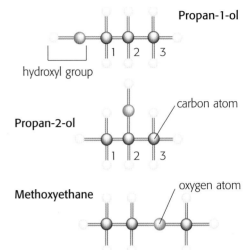

▲ The three isomers of C_3H_8O. Numbers 1–3 refer to the position of the carbon atoms.

Alcohol molecules that have two hydroxyl group in their molecules are called glycols. A few compounds have even more hydroxyl groups. For example, glycerol—$C_3H_5(OH)_3$—has three hydroxyl groups (*see* p. 48).

UNEVEN CHARGES

Oxygen atoms are very reactive. They pull on electrons more strongly than do the atoms of most other elements. The oxygen atom in an alcohol molecule pulls electrons away from the carbon and hydrogen atoms nearby. As a result, the oxygen atom becomes slightly

▶ Pure alcohol is made by distillation. In this process, a mixture containing alcohol is heated so the alcohol boils. The vapor is then turned back into a liquid by a water-cooled condenser.

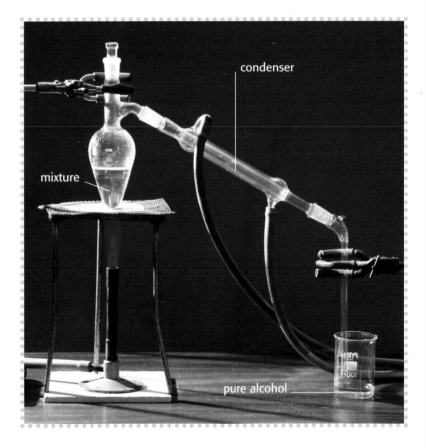

A Closer LOOK

Phenol

When a hydroxyl group (–OH) bonds to a benzene ring (*see* pp. 31–32), it forms a special alcohol. The compound is called a phenol. The simplest phenol is C_6H_5OH.

In a benzene ring, some electrons are spread evenly around the molecule. That makes a hydroxyl group behave differently in a phenol from how it does in an alcohol. The ring of shared electrons expands to include the oxygen atom (O) and holds it very tightly to the molecule. The bond between the oxygen atom and its hydrogen atom (H) becomes weak. The bond breaks easily. That produces two ions: H^+ and $C_6H_5O^-$. Compounds that split up in this way are called acids (*see* p. 44). Phenols are weak acids.

▲ *Phenol crystals have a pink color. They dissolve in water to make an acid called carbolic acid.*

▼ *When it is mixed with water, phenol becomes carbolic acid. In the past that was used in strong soaps.*

negatively charged. The hydrogen bonded to it has a slight positive charge. Opposite charges attract each other, so the hydrogen atom on one alcohol molecule is drawn toward the oxygen atom on the other. That creates a weak bond between the two molecules. This attraction is called a hydrogen bond. Many oxygen compounds form hydrogen bonds, including water (*see* vol. 1: pp. 51–52).

Hydrogen bonds hold alcohol molecules together more strongly. As a result, the boiling points of alcohols are higher than those of hydrocarbons without oxygen. The boiling point is the temperature at which the molecules in a liquid break free of each other and turn into a gas. Both methanol and ethanol are liquids in normal conditions. Without hydrogen bonds between their molecules, these alcohols would be gases.

The negative charge of the oxygen atom also affects the way alcohols react. For example, they react with oxygen to

Chemistry in Action

Antiseptics

Today, a surgeon's operating room is very clean. No one is allowed in unless they wash themselves and put on protective clothing. If any dirt got into a patient's body during an operation he or she might become very ill and die. The dirt contains tiny life-forms called bacteria, which infect the body and cause illness.

About 150 years ago, people did not understand these risks. People often died after operations, not because of the surgery itself but because of infections. In 1865, a British surgeon named Joseph Lister (1827 –1912) began using carbolic acid (phenol in water) to make operating rooms sterile (free of bacteria). The phenol was acidic enough to kill bacteria but it was also mild so it did not hurt the patient. Lister's idea led to the way surgery is performed today.

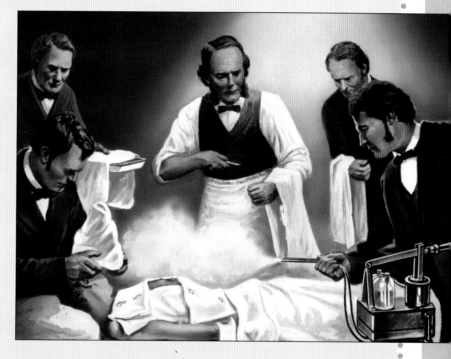

▲ Joseph Lister prepares to begin surgery in 1865. His assistant on the right is spraying carbolic acid (phenol and water) over the patient to kill any bacteria that might cause a dangerous infection.

make compounds called aldehydes and ketones (see pp. 49–50). Alcohols will also react with oxygen to form acidic compounds called carboxylic acids.

CARBOXYLIC ACIDS

Carboxylic acids have two functional groups. One of them is a hydroxyl (–OH), the group also found in alcohols and phenols. The other functional group is called a carbonyl (–CO). In this group, an oxygen atom is bonded to a carbon atom. The two atoms are connected by a double bond (see p. 11).

▶ Lime juice contains citric acid, a type of carboxylic acid. The citric acid is what gives limes and similar fruits their sharp tastes.

A Closer LOOK

Carboxylic acids

The main group of organic acids are called the carboxylic acids. They have a hydroxyl (–OH) and carbonyl (–CO) group bonded together. Some carboxylic acids have several of these groups.

Carboxylic acids split into ions. A hydrogen ion (H^+) breaks away from the rest of the molecule, which becomes a negatively charged carboxylate ion. For example, methanoic acid forms methanoate ions ($HCOO^-$).

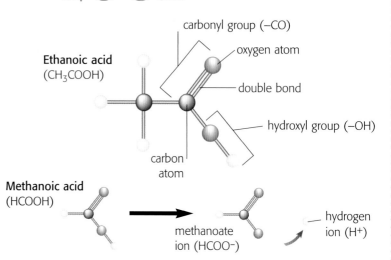

Ethanoic acid (CH_3COOH)

carbonyl group (–CO)

oxygen atom

double bond

hydroxyl group (–OH)

carbon atom

Methanoic acid (HCOOH)

methanoate ion ($HCOO^-$)

hydrogen ion (H^+)

In a carboxylic acid molecule, both of these functional groups are attached to the same carbon atom. Together they form a carboxyl group (–COOH).

COMMON ACIDS

Just like the alcohols and other organic compounds, carboxylic acids are named according to how many carbon atoms there are in their molecules (*see* box, p. 20). All their names end in *-oic*.

However, many carboxylic acids are found in foods or occur elsewhere in nature, and over the years they have been given other names. For example, vinegar contains ethanoic acid (CH_3COOH). This compound is also known as acetic acid. Methanoic acid (HCOOH) is also known as formic acid.

There are many other natural carboxylic acids. These include citric acid from lemons, oranges, and other citrus fruits. Lactic acid is made by muscles when they work hard. It is

this acid reacting with other compounds in the muscles that makes them ache and feel tired.

Longer carboxylic acid molecules are called fatty acids. They are found in milk, oils, and fats (*see* p. 48). For example, lauric acid occurs in coconut milk.

ACID REACTIONS

Carboxylic acids are made when alcohols react with oxygen (O_2). Ethanoic acid is made in nature as part of the same

▼ *The stings of fire ants contain formic acid (HCOOH). The acid causes painful blisters on the skin.*

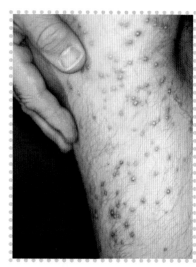

Chemistry in Action

Pickling

Food can be stored for a long time by pickling. Food is pickled in either vinegar (ethanoic acid) or strong alcohol (ethanol). The acid in vinegar stops bacteria on the food from growing. Food that has bacteria growing on it will go bad. The vinegar also soaks into the food giving it a strong flavor. Pickling in alcohol also gives the food a certain flavor. However, this time the food is preserved thanks to bacteria, which slowly turn the ethanol into ethanoic acid. This acid then stops the food from going bad.

▶ These pickles are small cucumbers that have been preserved in salty vinegar.

fermentation process that turns sugars into ethanol (C_2H_5OH). As we have seen, yeast makes the alcohol, but the changes do not end there. If the ethanol is exposed to the air, bacteria mixed into it will turn it into ethanoic acid. This reaction has the following equation:

$$C_2H_5OH + O_2 \rightarrow CH_3COOH + H_2O$$

That is why wine and other alcoholic beverages will begin to taste sour after being opened for a long time. They are slowly turning into vinegar!

Positively charged hydrogen ions (H^+) break off carboxylic acid molecules. That is why they are classed as acids. Acids are reactive compounds because they produce hydrogen ions. Acids react with other compounds to produce substances called salts (*see* vol. 3: pp. 26–27).

When it loses its hydrogen ion, the rest of the carboxylic acid becomes a negatively charged ion (*see* box, p. 44).

During a reaction, this ion forms a salt. The salts of carboxylic acids have names ending in -*oate*. When ethanoic acid (CH_3COOH) reacts with calcium hydroxide, $Ca(OH)_2$ it produces calcium ethanoate, $Ca(CH_3COO)_2$, and water (H_2O). The equation for this reaction looks like this:

$$2CH_3COOH + Ca(OH)_2 \rightarrow Ca(CH_3COO)_2 + H_2O$$

See Also ...
● *Types of Reactions, Vol. 3: pp. 22–35.*

Key Terms

- **Acid:** A compound that splits easily into a positively charged hydrogen ion and another negatively charged ion.
- **Benzene:** A ring of carbon atoms in which some electrons are shared by all atoms in the molecule.
- **Carbonyl:** A functional group in which an oxygen atom is connected to a carbon atom by a double bond.
- **Ion:** An atom or molecule that has lost or gained one or more electrons and has become electrically charged.

6 Other Organic Compounds

There are many types of functional groups, and each one gives organic compounds certain properties. As well as containing oxygen atoms, there are also functional groups that contain atoms of other elements.

There are many classes of organic compounds. A compound is formed when atoms of two or more elements bond together. Organic compounds are made up of mostly atoms of carbon (C) and hydrogen (H). Compounds containing only these elements are known as hydrocarbons (*see* p. 18). However, many organic molecules also contain atoms of other elements. Where these atoms bond

Many of nature's smells and tastes, such as the fragrance of flowers, are produced by organic compounds. Pleasant smells are from compounds containing oxygen, while foul-smelling compounds contain nitrogen or sulfur.

Key Terms

- **Compound:** Atoms of different elements bonded together.
- **Functional group:** A section of an organic molecule that gives it certain chemical properties.
- **Molecule:** Two or more atoms connected together.
- **Organic:** Describes a compound that is made of carbon and that generally also contains hydrogen.

to the hydrocarbon, they form a functional group. The functional group has an effect on the way that compound behaves. Organic compounds are classed according to their functional groups. There are many functional groups. This chapter looks at some of the groups containing oxygen atoms (O), nitrogen (N), sulfur (S), and chlorine (Cl).

ACID PLUS ALCOHOL

As we have seen, alcohol (*see* p. 39) and carboxylic acids (*see* p. 43) are types of organic compounds that are common in the natural world. They both have functional groups containing oxygen.

When an alcohol and carboxylic acid react, they form a compound called an ester. An ester forms when an alcohol's functional group reacts with the functional group of the acid. Alcohols have a hydroxyl functional group made from an oxygen and hydrogen atom (–OH; *see* p. 39). Carboxylic acids have a hydroxyl group, too, but they also have

---

A Closer LOOK

Esters

When alcohols react with carboxylic acids they form compounds called esters. An ester molecule has two halves, one side coming from the alcohol and the other from the acid. These two sections are connected by an oxygen atom. The side of the molecule that was originally from the acid contains a carbonyl group (–CO).

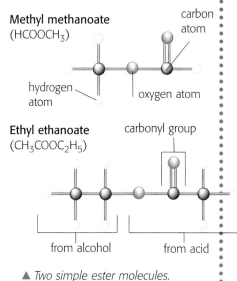

Methyl methanoate ($HCOOCH_3$)

Ethyl ethanoate ($CH_3COOC_2H_5$)

▲ *Two simple ester molecules.*

▼ The smell of pineapples is produced by an ester called ethyl butanoate.

a carbonyl group. That is a carbon atom connected to an oxygen atom by a double bond (*see* p. 11).

To make an ester, the alcohol loses a hydrogen atom from it hydroxyl group. The oxygen atom left behind attaches to the carbon atom in the acid's carbonyl group. The acid also loses its hydroxyl to form an ester. The hydroxyl group and hydrogen atom also bond together to make water (H_2O).

Like all organic compounds, esters are named according to how many carbon atoms they have (*see* p. 20). The simplest ester is methyl methanoate ($HCOOCH_3$). This compound is produced when methanol (CH_3OH) reacts with methanoic

Chemistry in Action

From fats to soaps

Vegetable oils and animal fats are complex ester compounds called triglycerides. They are formed when three large carboxylic acids bond to an alcohol called glycerol. The carboxylic acids in fats and oils are long-chained molecules. They are called fatty acids.

Soap is made from triglycerides. An alkali (*see* vol. 6: p. 16), such as sodium hydroxide (NaOH), is added to the esters. That makes each ester split into a glycerol and three fatty acids. The sodium forms compounds with the acids. These compounds are waxy solids and are filtered out and dried. Perfume and coloring is then added before the soap is pressed in bars.

▲ *Soap is made from the ester compounds in fats and oils.*

acid (HCOOH; also called formic acid). The equation for the reaction is:

$$HCOOH + CH_3OH$$
$$\rightarrow HCOOCH_3 + H_2O$$

The ester's name has two parts because its molecule is in two parts. The ester is named methyl methanoate. One side comes from the methanol. That has lost a hydrogen atom and becomes the methyl part of the ester. The section from the methanoic acid has lost its hydroxyl group. The section produced by that is called methanoate (*see* p. 45).

ODORS AND OILS

Most small ester compounds are liquids. These liquids evaporate easily (turn into a gas), and many of them have a distinctive smell. For example, the smell

A molecule of fat. The molecule has three fatty acids attached to a central glycerol molecule. Together they form a complex ester. The red spheres are the oxygen atoms holding the molecule together.

of a banana is an ester called isopentyl ethanoate. Many of the artificial flavors used in candy are esters. They are also added to perfumes (*see* box, p. 51).

Large ester compounds do not evaporate easily. Instead they are oily liquids and waxy solids. Some animal fats and vegetable oils are complex ester compounds. Such fats and oils are made up of three carboxylic acid molecules connected to an alcohol

A Closer LOOK

Aldehydes

There are two types of compounds that have just a carbonyl as their functional group. Aldehydes have this carbonyl at the end of each molecule. Ketones have carbonyls in the middle of each molecule (*see* box, p. 50). The carbonyl group is made up of an oxygen connected to a carbon atom by a double bond. It is a very reactive functional group.

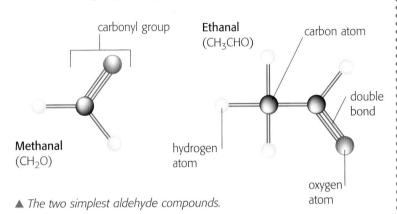

carbonyl group

Ethanal
(CH₃CHO)

carbon atom

double bond

Methanal
(CH₂O)

hydrogen atom

oxygen atom

▲ *The two simplest aldehyde compounds.*

called glycerol (*see* vol. 9: pp. 13–15). Glycerol molecules have three hydroxyl groups (–OH), and each one forms an ester with a large carboxylic acid, known as a fatty acid. Fatty acids may be saturated or unsaturated (*see* p. 23). Saturated molecules contain only single bonds, while unsaturated molecules have one or more double bonds. Most animal fats are saturated compounds; many vegetable oils are unsaturated fatty acids.

ALDEHYDES AND KETONES

There are two classes of organic compounds that have a single carbonyl (–CO) as their functional group. They are the aldehydes and ketones. Both classes of compounds are very similar. The only difference in their structures is that an aldehyde has a carbonyl group attached to the end of its molecule. A ketone has the same group attached in the middle of the molecule. These compounds are classed as two groups because the difference in their structure has an effect on their reactivity.

▲ *A dead giant squid is kept preserved in a tank of water and methanal, a type of aldehyde. Methanal, also known as formaldehyde, prevents the squid's body from decaying.*

Key Terms

- **Aldehyde:** A compound with a carbonyl group attached to the end of its molecule.
- **Carbonyl:** A functional group made by a carbon atom connected to an oxygen atom by a double bond.
- **Ester:** A compound formed when an alcohol reacts with a carboxylic acid.
- **Evaporate:** To turn from liquid to gas.

The names of aldehydes and ketones are based on how many carbon atoms they contain. Aldehydes have names that end in –al, while ketones have names ending in –one.

The simplest aldehyde is methanal (H_2CO). This compound is perhaps more familiar by its old name, formaldehyde. The simplest ketone is propanone (CH_3COCH_3). Again, this compound is also commonly referred to by its older name, acetone.

PHYSICAL PROPERTIES

Methanal is a volatile liquid. A volatile substance is one that changes into a gas easily. Methanal has a boiling point of just 69 degrees Fahrenheit (69°F; 21°C). That is about normal room temperature. On a hot day the compound boils away! Methanal has a very sharp and unpleasant odor.

Propanone is also a liquid. It boils at 133°F (56°C). Like other ketones, propanone has a sweet smell.

CARBONYL CHEMISTRY

Aldehydes and ketones are more reactive than most organic compounds because of the carbonyl group. The double bond holding the oxygen to the compound is very likely to break and form two single bonds. The oxygen atom pulls the electrons away from the carbon atom and gains a slight negative charge. Other

▲ Liquid ketones such as propanone are used as solvents— liquids that dissolve other compounds. For example, nail polish is waterproof and does not wash off in water. Nail-polish remover contains ketones, which can dissolve the nail polish and wash it away.

A Closer LOOK

Ketones

The simplest ketone has three carbon atoms. That is because a ketone has to have its carbonyl group located in the middle of the molecule. Apart from propanone, other ketone molecules have numbers in their names. These numbers show which carbon atom the carbonyl group is attached to.

Propanone
(CH_3COCH_3)

carbonyl group

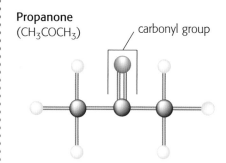

▲ A molecule of propanone.

Key Terms

- **Boiling point:** The temperature at which a liquid turns into a gas.
- **Ether:** Compound in which two hydrocarbon groups are joined by an oxygen atom.
- **Ketone:** A compound with a carbonyl group attached in the middle of its molecule.
- **Volatile:** Describes a liquid that evaporates (turns into a gas) easily.

molecules are attracted to this charge, and that is why the oxygen atom is so likely to be involved in a reaction.

An aldehyde is more reactive than a ketone because its carbonyl group is exposed at the end of the molecule. There it is bonded to one carbon atom and one hydrogen atom. As a result, the electrons are pulled very close to the oxygen atom. In a ketone, the carbonyl group is bonded between two carbon atoms. These larger atoms stop the oxygen atom from pulling the electrons quite so close. As a result, the aldehyde's oxygen atom has a stronger charge than a ketone's, and the aldehyde is more likely to react.

Aldehydes and ketones are halfway between alcohols and carboxylic acids. An alcohol can become an aldehyde or ketone by losing two hydrogen atoms. For example, methanol (CH_3OH) becomes methanal (H_2CO) through the reaction:

$$CH_3OH \rightarrow H_2CO + H_2$$

Methanal can be turned into methanoic acid (HCOOH) by adding oxygen (O_2). That reaction is as follows:

$$2H_2CO + O_2 \rightarrow 2HCOOH$$

ETHERS

An organic compound that has an oxygen atom bonded between two carbon atoms is called an ether. Ethers are made when two alcohols join together. During this reaction two hydrogen atoms (H) and an oxygen atom (O) are taken from the alcohol molecules and become a molecule of water (H_2O). The reaction

Chemistry in Action

Making perfumes

Several familiar odors and flavors are produced by ketone compounds. For example, the taste of cheese comes from complex ketones. Musk is another fragrant ketone. It is used to make expensive perfumes. Its odor comes from the compound muscone. Musk is used in perfumes because other fragrances, such as esters, can be mixed into it easily to make pleasant odors.

Natural musk is produced by a small type of deer. For many years, musk deer were hunted for their musk glands. Today the deer are very rare, and muscone is made in laboratories.

▲ Musk comes from a gland on the belly of a male musk deer. Males use it to mark their territory. Deer are sometimes killed for their musk.

▶ Many perfumes contain musk. Other fragrant chemicals are mixed into it.

▲ Methoxymethane is used to make the spray in aerosol cans.

Ethers

Ether molecules have two halves connected to each other by an oxygen atom. The molecules are named for these two sections. The last part of the name relates to the size and structure of the largest section. That section takes the name of its equivalent hydrocarbon. For example, if the section has two carbon atoms, it is called ethane. The smaller section's name is also based on its number of carbon atoms. However, an *–oxy* is added to show that it is connected to the larger section by an oxygen atom.

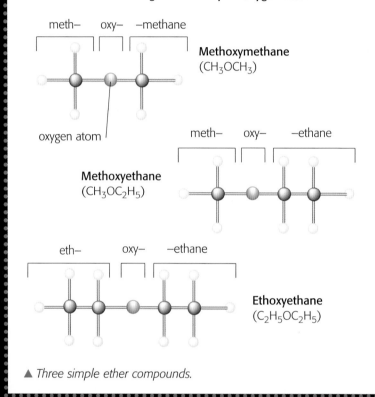

meth–   oxy–   –methane

Methoxymethane
(CH_3OCH_3)

oxygen atom

meth–   oxy–   –ethane

Methoxyethane
($CH_3OC_2H_5$)

eth–   oxy–   –ethane

Ethoxyethane
($C_2H_5OC_2H_5$)

▲ Three simple ether compounds.

is described as a dehydration because water is being removed from the alcohols as they are joined together.

The simplest ether compound is called methoxymethane (CH_3OCH_3). The molecule is named for the two sections on either side of the oxygen atom (*see* box above). Methoxymethane is made by dehydrating two molecules of methanol (CH_3OH). The reaction is as follows:

$$CH_3OH + CH_3OH \rightarrow CH_3OCH_3 + H_2O$$

▶ The flavor of aniseed is produced by a complex ether called anethole. The ether also flavors fennel and licorice.

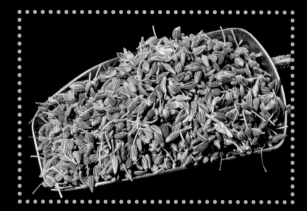

Chemistry in Action

Smelly sulfur

Sulfur is in the same group as oxygen in the periodic table (*see* vol. 7: pp. 36–47). Therefore, the two elements share similar properties. Like oxygen atoms (O), sulfur atoms (S) can form a total of two bonds. Sulfur forms organic compounds that are similar in structure to those formed by oxygen.

For example, thiols are sulfur's equivalent to alcohols. Instead of having an –OH group, thiols have an –SH group. Thiols have a rotten-egg odor. For example, the smell produced by a skunk (*right*) to repel attackers is butane-1-thiol (C_4H_9SH). Tiny amounts of that thiol are also added to natural gas to give it a distinctive smell.

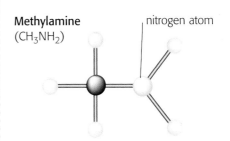

Because their oxygen atoms are bonded strongly to two carbons atoms, ethers are not very reactive. However, ethoxyethane ($C_2H_5OC_2H_5$) was used as the first anesthetic (*see* box, p. 54).

NITROGEN GROUP

An organic compound that contains a single nitrogen atom (N) is called an amine. Nitrogen atoms can form three bonds. In an amine all of them are single bonds.

The nitrogen atom sits at the center of the molecule, which is in three sections. In a simple amine, two of those sections might simply be hydrogen atoms. At least one of the sections is an alkyl group. An alkyl group is a section of hydrocarbon (see p. 24) that branches off another molecule or is attached to

▼ *The distinctive smell of fish is from an amine compound called trimethylamine.*

A Closer LOOK

Amines

An amine is an organic compound containing a nitrogen atom. Amines are similar to ammonia (NH_3; *see* vol. 7: pp. 24–35). An amine compound has hydrocarbons in place of at least one of the hydrogen atoms. Amines are reactive compounds. They are used to make certain dyes (*see* p. 36).

Methylamine (CH_3NH_2)   nitrogen atom

▲ *A molecule of methylamine, the simplest amine compound.*

a functional group. For example, the simplest alkyl group is a methyl ($-CH_3$). So the simplest amine is called methylamine (CH_3NH_2).

The nitrogen atom may be bonded to two alkyl groups, for example, a methyl and an ethyl ($-C_2H_5$). In this case the alkyl groups are listed alphabetically, so the molecule is named ethylmethylamine. When there are two methyl groups, it is dimethylamine. When there are three, then the name is trimethylamine.

ORGANIC HALIDES

The halogens are a very reactive group of elements (*see* vol. 7: pp. 48–59). They include fluorine (F), chlorine (Cl), and bromine (Br). These elements form compounds called organic halides.

In an organic halide, one or more halogen atoms is bonded to a carbon atom. The halogens take the place of the hydrogen atom, and in some organic halides there are no hydrogen atoms at all. The halides are named for the halogens in them. Bromocarbons contain bromine, while chlorofluorocarbons contain both chlorine and fluorine atoms.

In many ways organic halides are very similar to hydrocarbons. They have slightly higher melting and boiling points

A Closer LOOK

Chloromethanes

Chlorine forms four chloromethanes. These compounds have between one and four chlorine atoms (Cl) bonded to a single carbon atom. Chloromethane (CH_3Cl) has one chlorine atom. It is a poisonous gas. Dichloromethane (CH_2Cl_2) has two chlorine atoms. It is a colorless liquid often used as a pesticide. With three chlorine atoms, trichloromethane ($CHCl_3$) is better known as chloroform. It was one of the first anesthetics—a drug that makes people unconscious. Tetrachloromethane (CCl_4) has four chlorine atoms and no hydrogen atoms. It is used in dry cleaning.

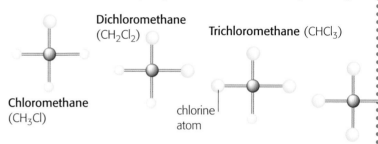

Dichloromethane (CH_2Cl_2)

Trichloromethane ($CHCl_3$)

Chloromethane (CH_3Cl)

chlorine atom

Tetrachloromethane (CCl_4)

▲ *The four chloromethane molecules.*

than corresponding hydrocarbons. The halogen atoms are much heavier than hydrogen atoms, so the molecules need to be hotter before they break apart.

Organic halides are also very stable compounds. Fluorine is the most reactive nonmetal element of all, and the other halogens are not far behind. The bonds their atoms form with carbon atoms are very strong. As a result the organic halides do not break down easily.

For many years chemists thought that certain organic halides were too stable to react in normal conditions. People have since released huge amounts into the air. However, we now know that these chemicals have been very destructive to the environment (*see* box, right).

Key Terms

- **Alkyl group:** A section of hydrocarbon chain attached to a functional group.
- **Amine:** An organic compound containing a single nitrogen atom.
- **Halide:** A compound containing a halogen atom, such as chlorine or iodine.

See Also ...

Nitrogen and Phosphorus,
Vol. 7: pp. 24–35.
Oxygen and Sulfur,
Vol. 7: pp. 36–47.

Chemistry in Action

Losing ozone

A group of organic halides are called the chlorofluorocarbons. This name is often shortened to CFC. CFC compounds contain fluorine (F) and chlorine (Cl) atoms attached to chains of carbon atoms. CFCs are very stable compounds because the bonds between the atoms are very strong. In normal conditions, such as those in your house, they never react. If CFCs are released into the air, they will stay there for a very long time without changing.

In the 20th century, CFC gases were used in many ways. They were used inside refrigerators and to make the spray in aerosol cans. Chemists thought that CFCs could be released into the air and would not cause any problems.

However, in 1974, Mario Molina (1943–), a Mexican chemist, discovered that CFCs were reacting with ozone in the atmosphere. Ozone is an allotrope (form; *see* p. 14) of oxygen. Most oxygen molecules have two atoms in them, making an O_2. Ozone has three atoms in an unstable O_3 molecule.

Ozone forms a layer high in the atmosphere that filters out dangerous radiation from the Sun. The CFCs are destroying the ozone layer and letting harmful radiation through the atmosphere. In 1987 CFCs were banned. The ozone layer is now slowly re-forming. CFCs have been replaced with other organic compounds. For example, aerosol cans now contain the ether methoxymethane (*see* p. 52).

◄ *A girl applies sunscreen. Having less ozone in the atmosphere means that it is easier to get sunburned.*

▶ *A satellite image of the hole in the ozone layer (purple).*

▲ *Old refrigerators that contain a CFC must have the gas removed.*

Polymers

Polymers are compounds made from long chains of smaller molecules. Polymers occur naturally in the world around us. They are also made from petrochemicals for use as plastics and to make clothing.

The world's main source of hydrocarbons is petroleum, or crude oil (*see* p. 18). Nine-tenths of the hydrocarbons in crude oil are turned into gasoline and other fuels (*see* p. 25).

What happens to the rest? Most of it is turned into compounds called polymers. Polymers are as varied as they are useful. They are used in everything from fighter planes to frying pans.

Plastic balls are made from polymer. Polymers can be made into any shape and are used in place of all types of naturally occurring materials, such as wood, stone, glass, china, and metals.

Key Terms

• **Compound:** A substance containing the atoms of two or more different elements.
• **Hydrocarbon:** An organic compound containing carbon and hydrogen atoms.
• **Molecule:** Two or more atoms connected together.
• **Organic:** Describes a compound that contains carbon and generally hydrogen but also atoms of other elements.

A Closer LOOK

Monomers

Polymers are chains of smaller molecules called monomers. A polymer may be made up of just one type of monomer. Such polymers are called homopolymers. (The word *homo* means "same.") Other polymers contain two or more types of monomers that are bonded alternately, one after the other. These polymers are called copolymers. (The word *co* means "together.")

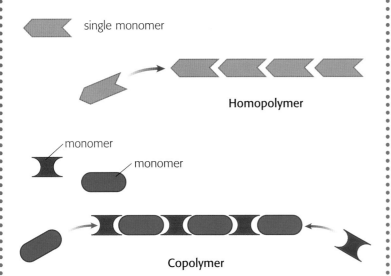

single monomer

Homopolymer

monomer

monomer

Copolymer

TYPES OF POLYMERS

There are many types of polymers. Some occur in nature (*see* box, p. 58), but people make most of the polymers around us from petrochemicals. Many polymers are known as plastics. They can be molded into any shape (*see* box, p. 59).

CHAINS OF MOLECULES

Polymers are very large molecules. They are made up of many smaller molecules that are connected into a chain. The smaller units are called monomers. The word *mono* means "alone," while *poly* means "many." So, a polymer is a compound that contains many monomers. Monomers form polymers in a process called polymerization.

▶ We use polymers every day. For example, in this shopping cart the cardboard and plastic packages are made from polymers. The food itself contains polymers, and even the cart's wheels are made from a polymer.

Other polymers are called rubbers. They are stretchy, or elastic, and can be bent out of shape easily but always spring back to their original form.

The properties of polymers are determined by the nature of their monomers and the way the chains are formed (*see* box, p. 61).

MAKING POLYMERS

Monomers can be made to polymerize (form into a polymer) through a number of reactions. Monomers that have double bonds, such as alkenes (*see* p. 23), are

▲ *Antique golf balls made from gutta percha, a natural plastic made from tree sap.*

polymerized by an addition reaction. These reactions occur when a double bond breaks and forms new single bonds.

The simplest polymer made in this way is polyethylene, known by chemists as polyethene. The monomer of this polymer is ethene (C_2H_4). Ethene has a double bond joining its two carbon atoms. During polymerization, the double bond breaks, and the carbon atoms from a long chain. Each carbon atom is bonded to two other carbon atoms and two hydrogen atoms.

Chemistry in Action

Natural polymers

Nature is full of polymers. The bodies of plants, such as the wood inside trees, are made from a polymer called cellulose. This compound is a chain of sugar monomers. Starch is another polymer made from sugars. It is the soft material in bread, potatoes, and rice.

Even genes, the coded instructions that control how living bodies grow, are a polymer. That polymer is called deoxyribonucleic acid (DNA). It is made using four monomers. Each gene is coded with a unique combination of these monomers (*see* vol. 9: pp. 25–29).

Rubber is also a natural polymer. It comes from latex, the sticky white sap of the rubber tree. Adding acid and salt separates the solid polymer from the liquid part of the sap. At this stage raw rubber is stringy, like the cheese on a pizza. A process called vulcanization makes the rubber much tougher (*see* box, p. 64).

◄ *Latex is tapped from a rubber tree. Rubber made from latex is now often replaced with similar polymers made from hydrocarbons.*

Chemistry in Action

What are plastics?

People use most of the polymers discussed in this chapter to make plastics. Plastics are very useful materials because they can be made into any shape. The word *plastic* comes from the Greek word for "mold."

Plastics have many advantages over other materials (*see* below). For example, plastics do not rust or corrode like metals. They can be made to be flexible, so they do not shatter like glass. They are also waterproof, unlike wood. Plastics are also good insulators—they do not carry an electric current. Electric cables are coated in plastic to make them safe to handle.

A few rubberlike natural polymers can be made into plastic, but plastics are really human-made materials. The first plastics were invented in the late 19th century. These early plastics were brittle (shattered easily) and expensive to make, so they were not used as widely as plastics are today. Plastics today are very inexpensive and are used in everything from spacecraft to shopping bags.

There are two types of plastics: thermoplastics and thermosets. The word *thermo* means "heat." A thermoplastic becomes softer and more moldable when it gets hot. It eventually melts and can be remolded into any shape. Polyethylene and PVC are thermoplastics.

A thermoset is the opposite of a thermoplastic. It gets harder as it is heated. Once it has hardened, a thermoset will not melt. Thermosets are molded into objects that need to stay rigid when hot (*see* p. 65). Polyester and rubber are thermosets.

Modern polymers versus traditional materials

Application	Polymer	Traditional material	Advantages of polymer
Molded objects	Polypropene	Metal	This plastic is rigid like metal but but much lighter. It can also be molded at lower temperatures.
Bottles	PET (Polyethylene terephthalate)	Glass	PET is lighter than glass and it does not shatter when dropped.
Windows	Polycarbonate	Glass	This polymer makes windows that will not shatter. However, it gets scratched more easily than glass.
Paints	Acrylic	Oil	Acrylic paints do not smell as strongly as oil paints and they do not crack when dry.
Clothes and fabrics	Nylon	Cotton and wool	Nylon is not damaged by heat and water and it can be woven into huge sheets.

Chemistry in Action

Artificial fibers

Our clothes are made from fibers that are woven together. For thousands of years, people used fibers made from natural polymers. For example, wool comes from the fur of sheep and goats, while cotton fibers are made from the fluff around the seeds of cotton plants.

These natural fibers are often quite short and they have to be spun together to make threads and yarns long enough for weaving. In the late 19th century, chemists developed ways of making stronger fibers that were made from much longer polymers.

The first artificial fiber was made from cellulose, the polymer in wood. Fabric made from cellulose is called rayon. In the 1930s, U.S. chemist Wallace Carothers (1896–1937) invented nylon. Nylon was a completely new polymer made from amines (nitrogen compounds; see p. 53). Nylon has become the most common artificial fiber. It can be made into a huge variety of objects, from silky sheets to the bristles of a brush.

▶ *A strand of nylon is drawn from a beaker full of the polymer.*

Polyethylene can be made into long, straight chains or branched networks. The straight chains produce a hard and stiff material. Objects made from branched chains are more flexible.

NAMING POLYMERS

Other polymers made by addition reactions include polypropene and polystyrene. They are named for their monomers with *poly–* added at the beginning. Other polymers have very long names almost too long to say! Instead these polymers are known by

◀ *Wet suits are made of neoprene. This is a waterproof rubber made by addition reactions.*

A Closer LOOK

Common polymers

You may have heard the names of some common polymers, such as PVC or polyethylene. These compounds and other polymers have a range of different properties. Many of their properties depend on the nature of their monomers. Monomers are the small units that join together to make a long chain. Many plastics are made from a mixture of polymers. Each polymer adds certain characteristics to the plastic.

Polymer	Monomer	Monomer structure	Properties of polymer
Polyethene (polyethylene)	Ethene	carbon, hydrogen	Polyethene makes flexible plastics. It is used in packaging and to insulate electrical wires.
Polypropene (polypropylene)	Propene		This polymer makes plastics that are similar to polyethene but slightly tougher and more expensive.
Polystyrene	Styrene	phenyl	This polymer is used to make styrofoam. It is also added to other polymers to make them waterproof.
PVC (polyvinyl chloride)	Chloroethene (vinyl chloride)	chlorine	PVC makes very tough plastics. They are not damaged by fire or strong chemicals and are good insulators.
Teflon (polytetrafluoroethene)	Tetrafluoroethene	fluorine	Teflon is a very slippery substance that is used in nonstick pans.

their initials. For example, PVC stands for polyvinyl chloride. Vinyl chloride is another name for chloroethene (C_2H_3Cl).

MIXING POLYMERS

Polymerization carries on until there are no monomers left. If a new monomer is then added, the chain grows again. This behavior makes it possible to produce copolymers made from two or more different monomers.

The properties of a copolymer depend on the different monomers that make it up. Ethene makes soft polymers, while polypropene is tougher. Styrene makes glassy polymers, while rubber polymers

Chemistry in Action

Too slippery to stick

Nonstick pans are coated in a polymer called Teflon. This name is short for polytetrafluoroethene. Teflon is the slipperiest solid known. That is why nothing sticks in a nonstick pan—all the food just slips off the coating of Teflon.

Teflon was invented by the DuPont company in 1938, the same U.S. organization that had invented nylon a few years earlier. As well as nonstick kitchenware, Teflon has many other uses. For example, spacesuits and other gear used by astronauts contain Teflon. Teflon is used to make Gore-Tex clothes. These are made from two layers of nylon with Teflon sandwiched in between. Gore-Tex clothes are waterproof in a very special way. They stop rainwater from getting in, but the wearer's sweat can pass out in the other direction.

▲ *The inside of a nonstick frying pan is coated with a layer of Teflon. The Teflon is so slippery that even burned food will not stick to it.*

are elastic. Chemists can blend these monomers to produce a polymer with just the correct amount of each property. Copolymers can be made from blocks of each monomer, or they can be arranged randomly. Polymers can also be produced with a precise arrangement of monomers. For example, two types of monomers could be arranged one after the other. However, polymers like that are more expensive to produce.

Acrylic fiber is an example of a copolymer. It is a blend of two esters of certain acrylic acids—very reactive types of carboxylic acids (*see* p. 44).

CONDENSATION POLYMERS
Some monomers do not form polymers by addition reactions. Instead they polymerize with a condensation reaction. This reaction produces a molecule of water (H_2O) as the monomers bond together.

Nylon, polyester, and the natural polymers cellulose and starch (*see* box, p. 58) are condensation polymers. Their monomers have two or more

▼ *Large sewer pipes made from PVC. PVC makes tough objects that do not corrode or become damaged easily.*

functional groups. The monomers join together when the functional groups on each monomer react and form bonds.

The monomers have at least one more functional group, which is not involved in holding the polymer together. These free groups can form bonds with monomers on different polymers. That creates crosslinks between several polymer chains and makes a very strong network.

POLYMER PROPERTIES

When you look at a plastic cup, a rubber ball, or a nylon rope you cannot see the polymers inside them. The polymers are obviously far too small to see. If you

could see them, they would not all look the same. For example a plastic cup is very different from a rubber ball. That is because their polymer chains are arranged differently.

The properties of an object made from a polymer depend on how the polymers are arranged. The simplest arrangement is to have polymers that are unbranched

A versatile material?

You would be right to think that plastic is a very useful type of material. After all it can be made into just about anything. But what happens when we put plastic in the garbage? One of the properties of plastic is that it does not decay easily. So plastics buried along with other garbage remain unchanged for many thousands of years.

Other materials, such as metal or wood, can be recycled or reused. Plastic is more difficult to recycle. Thermosets cannot be melted down at all, and a mixture of different thermoplastics must be separated out before they can be remolded.

▶ *A man pulls a huge load of empty plastic bottles. Waste plastic does not weigh very much but it takes up a huge amount of space.*

and form straight chains. The chains may be many thousands or even millions of atoms in length. A sample of these polymers will contain chains with a wide range of lengths.

Unbranched, straight polymers are packed close together. Some even form crystals (see vol. 2: p. 47). Polymers like that make stiff materials. They do not change shape easily because the polymers inside are packed too closely to move around much.

However, when a sample of this material is stretched, the polymers slip past one another. As a result, the sample becomes longer. When the stretching stops, the polymers stay in their new position, and the sample keeps its new stretched shape (see box, p. 65). Materials that behave like this are said to be plastic.

A branched polymer has side chains along its main chain. The chains stop polymers from packing together closely. As a result, the polymers are more flexible. Addition polymers, such as polyethylene, can be formed as either straight or branched chains.

COILS AND CROSSLINKS

Rubbers are polymers that have coiled chains. When they are stretched, the coils straighten and become longer.

▲ Styrofoam is polystyrene pumped full of air bubbles.

Chemistry in Action

Vulcanization

When it is first made, rubber is a stretchy gumlike material. To make it into a useful elastic material, which can be used to make tires, soles for shoes, and countless other things, the rubber must be vulcanized. Vulcanizing adds crosslinks between the rubber's polymers. In the most common vulcanization process, sulfur is added to the rubber and heated. A sulfur (S) atom bonds to a carbon (C) atom on two polymers. That creates a C–S–C crosslink between chains. Adding more crosslinks makes the rubber even tougher.

◀ Tires made from vulcanized rubber are very tough, and that makes them difficult to dispose of. In the state of New York alone, 18 million used tires are thrown away each year.

Key Terms

- **Bond:** An attraction between atoms.
- **Crosslink:** A bond between two polymers.
- **Crystal:** A solid made of regular repeating patterns of atoms.
- **Elastic:** Describes substances that return to their original shape after being stretched.
- **Plastic:** Describes substances that change shape permanently after being stretched.

See ALSO ...
- *The Solid State, Vol. 2: pp. 46–57.*
- *Chemistry in Industry, Vol. 10: pp. 4–21.*

A Closer LOOK

Plastic or elastic?

The stretchiness of plastics, rubber, and other materials made from polymers depends on how their polymers are arranged.

Before stretching	During stretching	After stretching
unbranched and straight chains	Polymers slip a little.	Polymers stay stretched.
branched chains	Polymers slip easily.	Polymers stay stretched.
coiled chains	Polymers lengthen and slip past each other.	Polymers shorten again but the shape is stretched.
crosslinked coils	Coils lengthen but do not slip past each other.	Polymers spring back to original shape.
crosslinked straight chain	Polymers move only very slightly.	Polymers return to original shape.

However, once the stretching ends, the coiled chains spring back to their original shape. Polymers that behave like that are described as being elastic.

However, untreated rubber behaves like a plastic as well. Some of the polymers slip past each other, causing the rubber to stretch permanently. Adding crosslinks between the coils stops that from happening and makes the rubber completely elastic. The process that adds crosslinks to rubber is called vulcanization (*see* box, p. 64).

THERMOSETS

Polymers with lots of crosslinks make very rigid materials. For the material to break or change shape, the bonds in the crosslinks must be broken. Many polymers form crosslinks when they are heated. These compounds are called thermosets.

Thermosets are used to make molded objects. The powdered ingredients of the polymer are packed into a mold and heated. The heat makes the thermoset polymers form. The heat also causes crosslinks to connect the polymers making the object very rigid.

▲ *An antique radio made of bakelite. Bakelite was one of the first thermosets to be invented.*

More Information

BOOKS

Atkins, P. W. *The Periodic Kingdom: A Journey into the Land of Chemical Elements.* New York, NY: Basic Books, 1997.

Bendick, J., and Wiker, B. *The Mystery of the Periodic Table (Living History Library).* Bathgate, ND: Bethlehem Books, 2003.

Berg, J., Stryer, L., and Tymoczko, J. *Biochemistry.* New York, NY: W. H. Freeman, 2002.

Brown, T., Burdge, J., Bursten, B., and LeMay, E. *Chemistry: The Central Science.* 10th ed. Englewood Cliffs, NJ: Prentice Hall, 2005.

Cobb, C., and Fetterolf, M. L. *The Joy of Chemistry: The Amazing Science of Familiar Things.* Amherst, NY: Prometheus Books, 2005.

Cox, M., and Nelson, D. *Lehninger's Principles of Biochemistry.* 4th ed. New York, NY: W. H. Freeman, 2004.

Davis, M. *Modern Chemistry.* New York, NY: Henry Holt, 2000.

Herr, N., and Cunningham, J. *Hands-on Chemistry Activities with Real Life Applications.* Hoboken, NJ: Jossey-Bass, 2002.

Houck, Clifford C., and Post, Richard. *Chemistry: Concepts and Problems.* Hoboken, NJ: Wiley, 1996.

Karukstis, K. K., and Van Hecke, G. R. *Chemistry Connections: The Chemical Basis of Everyday Phenomena.* Burlington, MA: Academic Press, 2003.

LeMay, E. *Chemistry: Connections to Our Changing World.* New York, NY: Prentice Hall (Pearson Education), 2000.

Oxlade, C. *Elements and Compounds.* Chicago, IL: Heinemann, 2002.

Poynter, M. *Marie Curie: Discoverer of Radium (Great Minds of Science).* Berkeley Heights, NJ: Enslow Publishers, 2007.

Saunders, N. *Fluorine and the Halogens.* Chicago, IL: Heinemann Library, 2005.

Shevick, E., and Wheeler, R. *Great Scientists in Action: Early Life, Discoveries, and Experiments.* Carthage, IL: Teaching and Learning Company, 2004.

Stwertka, A. *A Guide to the Elements.* New York, NY: Oxford University Press, 2002.

Tiner, J. H. *Exploring the World of Chemistry: From Ancient Metals to High-Speed Computers.* Green Forest, AZ: Master Books, 2000.

Trombley, L., and Williams, F. *Mastering the Periodic Table: 50 Activities on the Elements.* Portland, ME: Walch, 2002.

Walker, P., and Wood, E. *Crime Scene Investigations: Real-life Science Labs for Grades 6–12.* Hoboken, NJ: Jossey-Bass, 2002.

Wertheim, J. *Illustrated Dictionary of Chemistry* (Usborne Illustrated Dictionaries). Tulsa, OK: Usborne Publishing, 2000.

Wilbraham, A., et al. *Chemistry.* New York, NY: Prentice Hall (Pearson Education), 2000.

Woodford, C., and Clowes, M. *Routes of Science: Atoms and Molecules.* San Diego, CA: Blackbirch Press, 2004.

WEB SITES

The Art and Science of Bubbles
www.sdahq.org/sdakids/bubbles
*Information and activities
about bubbles.*

Chemical Achievers
www.chemheritage.org/classroom/
chemach/index.html
*Biographical details about leading
chemists and their discoveries.*

The Chemistry of Batteries
www.science.uwaterloo.ca/~cchieh/
cact/c123/battery.html
Explanation of how batteries work.

The Chemistry of Chilli Peppers
www.chemsoc.org/exemplarchem/
entries/mbellringer
*Fun site giving information on the
chemistry of chilli peppers.*

The Chemistry of Fireworks
library.thinkquest.org/15384/
chem/chem.htm
*Information on the chemical
reactions that occur when
a firework explodes.*

The Chemistry of Water
www.biology.arizona.edu/
biochemistry/tutorials/chemistry/
page3.html
*Chemistry of water and other
aspects of biochemistry.*

Chemistry: The Periodic Table Online
www.webelements.com
Detailed information about elements.

Chemistry Tutor
library.thinkquest.org/2923
*A series of Web pages that help
with chemistry assignments.*

Chem4Kids
www.chem4Kids.com
*Includes sections on matter, atoms,
elements, and biochemistry.*

Chemtutor Elements
www.chemtutor.com/elem.htm
*Information on a selection of
the elements.*

Eric Weisstein's World of Chemistry
scienceworld.wolfram.com/
chemistry
*Chemistry information divided into
eight broad topics, from chemical
reactions to quantum chemistry.*

General Chemistry Help
chemed.chem.purdue.edu/genchem
*General information on chemistry
plus movie clips of key concepts.*

Molecular Models
chemlabs.uoregon.edu/
GeneralResources/models/
models.html
*A site that explains the use
of molecular models.*

New Scientist
www.newscientist.com/home.ns
*Online science magazine providing
general news on scientific
developments.*

Periodic Tables
www.chemistrycoach.com/periodic_
tables.htm#Periodic%20Tables
*A list of links to sites that have
information on the periodic table.*

The Physical Properties of Minerals
mineral.galleries.com/minerals/
physical.htm
Methods for identifying minerals.

Understanding Our Planet Through
Chemistry
minerals.cr.usgs.gov/gips/
aii-home.htm
*Site that shows how chemists
and geologists use analytical
chemistry to study Earth.*

Scientific American
www.sciam.com
*Latest news on developments
in science and technology.*

Snowflakes and Snow Crystals
www.its.caltech.edu/~atomic/
snowcrystals
*A guide to snowflakes, snow
crystals, and other ice
phenomena.*

Virtual Laboratory: Ideal Gas Laws
zebu.uoregon.edu/nsf/piston.html
*University of Oregon site showing
simulation of ideal gas laws.*

What Is Salt?
www.saltinstitute.org/15.html
Information on common salt.

Periodic Table

The periodic table organizes all the chemical elements into a simple chart according to the physical and chemical properties of their atoms. The elements are arranged by atomic number from 1 to 116. The atomic number is based on the number of protons in the nucleus of the atom. The atomic mass is the combined mass of protons and neutrons in the nucleus. Each element has a chemical symbol that is an abbreviation of its name. In some cases, such as potassium,

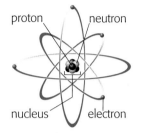

Atomic structure

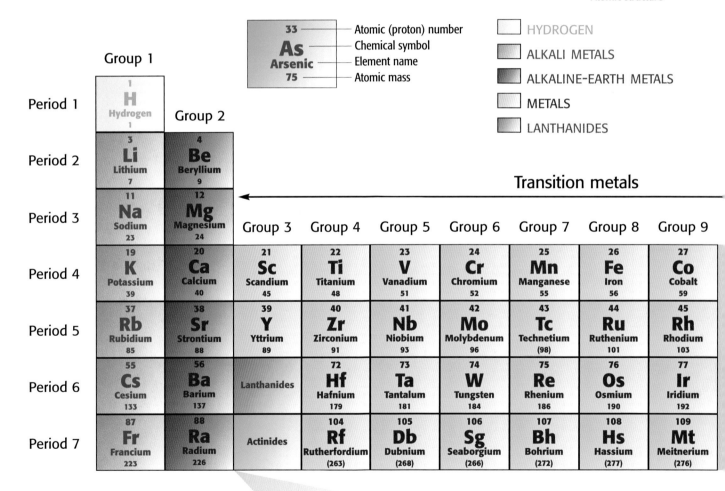

33	Atomic (proton) number
As	Chemical symbol
Arsenic	Element name
75	Atomic mass

- HYDROGEN
- ALKALI METALS
- ALKALINE-EARTH METALS
- METALS
- LANTHANIDES

Transition metals

Group 1

Period 1 — 1 H Hydrogen 1

Group 2

Period 2 — 3 Li Lithium 7 | 4 Be Beryllium 9

Period 3 — 11 Na Sodium 23 | 12 Mg Magnesium 24

Group 3 | Group 4 | Group 5 | Group 6 | Group 7 | Group 8 | Group 9

Period 4 — 19 K Potassium 39 | 20 Ca Calcium 40 | 21 Sc Scandium 45 | 22 Ti Titanium 48 | 23 V Vanadium 51 | 24 Cr Chromium 52 | 25 Mn Manganese 55 | 26 Fe Iron 56 | 27 Co Cobalt 59

Period 5 — 37 Rb Rubidium 85 | 38 Sr Strontium 88 | 39 Y Yttrium 89 | 40 Zr Zirconium 91 | 41 Nb Niobium 93 | 42 Mo Molybdenum 96 | 43 Tc Technetium (98) | 44 Ru Ruthenium 101 | 45 Rh Rhodium 103

Period 6 — 55 Cs Cesium 133 | 56 Ba Barium 137 | Lanthanides | 72 Hf Hafnium 179 | 73 Ta Tantalum 181 | 74 W Tungsten 184 | 75 Re Rhenium 186 | 76 Os Osmium 190 | 77 Ir Iridium 192

Period 7 — 87 Fr Francium 223 | 88 Ra Radium 226 | Actinides | 104 Rf Rutherfordium (263) | 105 Db Dubnium (268) | 106 Sg Seaborgium (266) | 107 Bh Bohrium (272) | 108 Hs Hassium (277) | 109 Mt Meitnerium (276)

rare-earth elements

— Lanthanides

| 57 La Lanthanum 39 | 58 Ce Cerium 140 | 59 Pr Praseodymium 141 | 60 Nd Neodymium 144 | 61 Pm Promethium (145) |

— Actinides

| 89 Ac Actinium 227 | 90 Th Thorium 232 | 91 Pa Protactinium 231 | 92 U Uranium 238 | 93 Np Neptunium (237) |

the symbol is an abbreviation of its Latin name ("K" stands for *kalium*). The name by which the element is commonly known is given in full underneath the symbol. The last item in the element box is the atomic mass. This is the average mass of an atom of the element.

Scientists have arranged the elements into vertical columns called groups and horizontal rows called periods. Elements in any one group all have the same number of electrons in their outer shell and have similar chemical properties. Periods represent the increasing number of electrons it takes to fill the inner and outer shells and become stable. When all the spaces have been filled (Group 18 atoms have all their shells filled) the next period begins. Further explanation of the periodic table is given in Volume 5.

ACTINIDES

NOBLE GASES

NONMETALS

METALLOIDS

Group 18

Group 10	Group 11	Group 12	Group 13	Group 14	Group 15	Group 16	Group 17	He 2 Helium 4
			5 B Boron 11	6 C Carbon 12	7 N Nitrogen 14	8 O Oxygen 16	9 F Fluorine 19	10 Ne Neon 20
			13 Al Aluminum 27	14 Si Silicon 28	15 P Phosphorus 31	16 S Sulfur 32	17 Cl Chlorine 35	18 Ar Argon 40
28 Ni Nickel 59	29 Cu Copper 64	30 Zn Zinc 65	31 Ga Gallium 70	32 Ge Germanium 73	33 As Arsenic 75	34 Se Selenium 79	35 Br Bromine 80	36 Kr Krypton 84
46 Pd Palladium 106	47 Ag Silver 108	48 Cd Cadmium 112	49 In Indium 115	50 Sn Tin 119	51 Sb Antimony 122	52 Te Tellurium 128	53 I Iodine 127	54 Xe Xenon 131
78 Pt Platinum 195	79 Au Gold 197	80 Hg Mercury 201	81 Tl Thallium 204	82 Pb Lead 207	83 Bi Bismuth 209	84 Po Polonium (209)	85 At Astatine (210)	84 Rn Radon (222)
110 Ds Darmstadtium (281)	111 Rg Roentgenium (280)	112 Uub Ununbium (285)	113 Uut Ununtrium (284)	114 Uuq Ununquadium (289)	115 Uup Ununpentium (288)	116 Uuh Ununhexium (292)		

artificial elements

62 Sm Samarium 150	63 Eu Europium 152	64 Gd Gadolinium 157	65 Tb Terbium 159	66 Dy Dysprosium 163	67 Ho Holmium 165	68 Er Erbium 167	69 Tm Thulium 169	70 Yb Ytterbium 173	71 Lu Lutetium 175
94 Pu Plutonium (244)	95 Am Americium (243)	96 Cm Curium (247)	97 Bk Berkelium (247)	98 Cf Californium (251)	99 Es Einsteinium (252)	100 Fm Fermium (257)	101 Md Mendelevium (258)	102 No Nobelium (259)	103 Lr Lawrencium (260)

Glossary

acid Substance that dissolves in water to form hydrogen ions (H^+). Acids are neutralized by alkalis and have a pH below 7.

adsorption The process of molecules becoming attached to a surface.

alcohol A compound formed when a hydroxide ion (OH^-) replaces a hydrogen atom on a hydrocarbon chain or an aromatic ring.

aldehyde A compound with a carbonyl group attached to the end of its molecule.

aliphatic compound An organic compound that has an open-chain structure, such as an alkane.

alkali Substance that dissolves in water to form hydroxide ions (OH^-). Alkalis have a pH greater than 7 and will react with acids to form salts.

alkane A hydrocarbon chain in which all atoms are connected by single bonds.

alkene A hydrocarbon chain in which at least two carbon atoms are connected by a double bond.

alkyne A hydrocarbon chain in which two carbon atoms are joined by a triple bond.

allotrope A different form of an element in which the atoms are arranged in a different structure.

arene A type of hydrocarbon compound that has ringed molecules.

aromatic Describes a compound that contains one or more benzene rings.

atom The smallest independent building block of matter. All substances are made of atoms.

atomic mass number The number of protons and neutrons in an atom's nucleus.

atomic number The number of protons in a nucleus.

benzene A ring of carbon atoms in which electrons are shared by all atoms in the molecule.

bond A chemical connection between atoms.

by-product A substance that is produced when another material is made.

carbohydrate One of a group of compounds that includes sugars, starch, and cellulose. Some are essential in turning food to energy. Others are energy stores in plants, and still more build plant and animal cell membranes.

carbonyl A functional group in which an oxygen atom is connected to a carbon atom by a double bond.

catalyst Substance that speeds up a chemical reaction but is left unchanged at the end of the reaction.

chemical equation Symbols and numbers that show how reactants change into products during a chemical reaction.

chemical formula The letters and numbers that represent a chemical compound, such as "H_2O" for water.

chemical reaction The reaction of two or more chemicals (the reactants) to form new chemicals (the products).

chemical symbol The letters that represent a chemical, such as "Cl" for chlorine or "Na" for sodium.

combustion The reaction that causes burning. Combustion is generally a reaction with oxygen in the air.

compound Substance made from more than one element and that has undergone a chemical reaction.

copolymer Polymer made from two or more different types of polymer.

covalent bond Bond in which atoms share one or more electrons.

cracking Process by which products of fractional oil distillation are broken down into simpler hydrocarbons.

crosslink A bond between two polymers.

dissolve To form a solution.

electron A tiny, negatively charged particle that moves around the nucleus of an atom.

element A material that cannot be broken up into simpler ingredients. Elements contain only one type of atom.

energy level Electron shells represent different energy levels. Those closest to the nucleus have the lowest energy.

ester A compound formed when an alcohol reacts with a carboxylic acid.

ether Compound in which two hydrocarbon molecules are connected by a single oxygen atom.

evaporation The change of state from a liquid to a gas when the liquid is at a temperature below its boiling point.

fractional distillation The process of heating crude oil to separate different hydrocarbon components.

fullerenes Ball- or tube-shaped allotropes of carbon made of hexagonal or pentagonal rings of carbon atoms.

functional group A section of an organic molecule that gives it certain chemical properties.

gas State in which particles are not joined and are free to move in any direction.

greenhouse gases Gases such as carbon dioxide and methane that trap heat in Earth's atmosphere.

halide A compound containing a halogen atom, such as chlorine or iodine.

homopolymer Polymer made from one type of monomer.

hydrocarbon Term for organic compounds that contain only carbon and hydrogen.

hydrogen bond A weak dipole attraction that always involves a hydrogen atom.

hydrolysis The process by which a molecule splits after reacting with a molecule of water.

hydroxyl A functional group (–OH) made up of an oxygen and a hydrogen atom.

inorganic A compound that is not organic.

intermolecular bonds The bonds that hold molecules together. These bonds are weaker than those between atoms in a molecule.

intramolecular bond Strong bond between atoms in a molecule.

ion An atom that has lost or gained one or more electrons.

ionic bond Bond in which one atom gives one or more electrons to another atom.

ionization The formation of ions by adding or removing electrons from atoms.

isomer A substance with the same chemical formula as another compound but which has a different structural arrangement of its atoms. It may also react differently.

ketone A compound with a carbonyl group attached in the middle of its molecule.

liquid Substance in which particles are loosely bonded and are able to move freely around each other.

matter Anything that can be weighed.

melting point The temperature at which a solid changes into a liquid. When a liquid changes into a solid, this same temperature is called the freezing point.

mixture Matter made from different types of substances that are not physically or chemically bonded together.

mole The amount of any substance that contains the same number of atoms as in 12 grams of carbon-12 atoms. This number is 6.022×10^{23}.

molecule Two or more joined atoms that have a unique shape and size.

monomer Monomers are molecules that join to form long chains called polymers.

neutron One of the particles that make up the nucleus of an atom. Neutrons do not have any electric charge.

nucleus The central part of an atom. The nucleus contains protons and neutrons. the exception is hydrogen, which contains only one proton.

organic A compound that is made of carbon and hydrogen.

organic acids Family of organic compounds that include the carboxylic acids and fatty acids, which both contain a –COOH group. Like inorganic acids they produce hydrogen ions (H^+).

oxidation The addition of oxygen to a compound.

oxidation state A number used to describe how many electrons an atom has lost or gained.

petrochemicals Organic chemicals that are made from petroleum or natural gas.

phenol An alcohol formed by the attachment of an –OH group to an aromatic ring.

plastic An organic polymer that can be molded or shaped into objects or films by heat.

polymerization The process that makes monomers join together to form polymers.

pressure The force produced by pressing on something.

products The new substance or substances created by a chemical reaction.

proton A positively charged particle found in an atom's nucleus.

reactants The ingredients necessary for a chemical reaction.

relative atomic mass A measure of the mass of an atom compared with the mass of another atom. The values used are the same as those for atomic mass.

relative molecular mass The sum of all the atomic masses of the atoms in a molecule.

salt A compound made from positive and negative ions that forms when an alkali reacts with an acid.

saturated hydrocarbon A hydrocarbon molecule in which all the carbon atoms are bonded to four other atoms. An unsaturated molecule contains double or triple bonds between carbon atoms.

shell The orbit of an electron. Each shell can contain a specific number of electrons and no more.

solid State of matter in which particles are held in a rigid arrangement.

solute The substance that dissolves in a solvent.

solution A mixture of two or more elements or compounds in a single phase (solid, liquid, or gas).

solvent The liquid that solutes dissolve in.

specific heat capacity The amount of heat required to change the temperature of a specified amount of a substance by 1°C (1.8°F).

state The form that matter takes—either a solid, a liquid, or a gas.

subatomic particles Particles that are smaller than an atom.

temperature A measure of how fast molecules are moving.

thermoplastic A type of polymer that becomes soft when heated such that it can be molded into shapes.

thermoset A type of polymer that hardens when it is heated and will not melt.

triglyceride A major component of fats. They are made from three fatty acids and a glycerol molecule. Triglycerides provide a concentrated food energy store in organisms.

valence electrons The electrons in the outer shell of an atom.

van der Waals forces Short-lived forces between atoms and molecules.

viscous Describes a liquid that is not very runny and flows slowly.

volatile Describes a liquid that evaporates easily.

voltage The force that pushes electrons through an electric circuit.

volume The space that a solid, liquid, or gas occupies.

vulcanization The process of adding crosslinks between rubber's polymers. This makes the rubber tougher.

zeolite A silicate mineral that is used as a catalyst in the cracking of oil.

Index

solids, continued
crystalline *see* crystalline; crystals
freezing **2**:55, 60–61, 63, 64
intermolecular force **2**:7–8
ionic **2**:52–53
melting **1**:9–11; **2**:10, 55, 59, 60, 63, 64; **4**:15
metallic **2**:50–52
molecular **2**:52, 55, 56
particles **1**:9
properties **2**:46–56
sublimation **2**:56–57
solubility **2**:39–43
solute **1**:15; **2**:35–44; **3**:26
solution **1**:14, 15; **2**:34–44, 47, 49, 51–52; **3**:25–26; **10**:36, 37
Solvay process **10**:14, 16
solvent extraction **10**:27–28
solvents **1**:15; **2**:29, 35–44, 45; **3**:26; **8**:50; **10**:49–50
nonpolar **2**:40; **9**:12–13
polar **2**:40; **9**:12; **10**:50
soot **7**:12; **8**:9, 12
specific heat capacity **4**:21
spectroscopy **5**:13–14; **6**:35; **10**:21
spontaneous reaction **3**:45–46; **4**:29, 35, 41, 52; **7**:25, 40
stability **3**:12–13, 15, 17; **5**:8–9, 45, 53; **6**:15, 24, 37; **8**:10, 33, 35
stainless steel **6**:44, 59; **10**:36
stalactites **7**:20; **10**:46, 48
stalagmites **7**:20; **10**:46, 48
Standard Temperature and Pressure (STP) **2**:13; **5**:32
starch **4**:61; **8**:58, 62; **9**:8–9, 10–11
stars **1**:4, 64–65; **5**:4; **7**:4–5, 11
steam *see* water vapor
steel **2**:34, 51, 52; **5**:40, 42; **6**:12, 13, 27, 41, 43, 47, 57, 58–59; **7**:20; **8**:14; **10**:37
steroids **9**:19
strong nuclear force **3**:59
strontium **5**:13, 31, 38–39; **6**:22–29
styrene **8**:61
subatomic particles *see* particles
sublimation **2**:56–57
substitution **10**:29
substrate **4**:63–64, 65
sucrose **9**:5, 7

sugar **3**:8–9, 30; **4**:57, 61–62; **8**:6, 40, 45, 58; **9**:5–11, 33–34
sulfa drugs **10**:56–57, 58, 60
sulfide **5**:34
sulfur **1**:5, 46; **2**:52; **5**:10, 11, 15, 16, 30, 31, 44, 46–49; **7**:36–37, 42–47; **8**:6, 14, 46, 53; **9**:4, 5
allotropes **5**:46–48, 49
sulfuric acid **5**:49; **7**:46–47; **10**:15–16
Sun **1**:4, 36, 42, 64; **2**:11; **3**:9, 30, 58, 63, 64; **7**:60; **8**:55; **9**:43; **10**:7–8, 40
superconductor **6**:38, 61
superfluids **7**:62
supernovas **1**:64–65; **5**:4
surface tension **2**:26–30
surfactant **10**:50
suspension **2**:34, 44–45
symbiosis **7**:26
synthesizing reaction **9**:46–65
synthetic fibers **8**:59–60; **10**:5, 12

T
talc **10**:42
taste **9**:4, 5
technetium **5**:22–23
teeth **1**:13; **2**:37; **6**:28
teflon **7**:50; **8**:61, 62; **10**:12
telluric screw **5**:16–17, 59
tellurium **5**:16–17, 31, 54, 59; **6**:60–65
temperature **1**:8; **2**:18, 41, 59; **3**:38–39, 41, 47–48; **4**:5, 6, 12–15, 21, 44; **9**:34
Brownian motion **2**:8
and pressure **2**:14, 18–21, 62–63
and reaction rate **4**:44–55
and solubility **2**:40, 43
states of matter **2**:10–11
see also boiling point; freezing point; heat; melting point
thallium **6**:30–35
thermal analysis **10**:21
thermal energy **9**:31
thermistor **6**:65
thermite process **6**:34
thermochemistry **3**:36
thermocouple **4**:14
thermodynamics **3**:36, 45; **4**:17, 29, 36–41
thermometer **2**:55; **4**:14; **5**:41; **6**:49, 65
thermophiles **7**:43
thermoplastics **8**:59, 63

thermosets **8**:59, 63, 65
thiols **5**:49; **7**:45; **8**:53
thorium **1**:57, 60–61; **3**:62; **5**:31, 61, 63–64; **7**:65
tin **1**:50; **5**:11, 35, 39, 41–42; **6**:4–5, 13, 36–41; **8**:14; **10**:31, 32, 37
titanium **1**:21; **6**:42–59; **10**:35
titration **3**:32
TNT (explosive) **8**:34
topaz **10**:42
toxins **5**:58; **9**:22
trace elements **9**:4; **10**:18
transcription **9**:52, 56–59
transfer RNA (tRNA) **9**:26, 59, 60
transgenic organisms **9**:61–64
transistor **6**:64
transition metals **5**:24–25, 28, 29, 35, 39–41; **6**:42–59
transition series **6**:46–47
translation **4**:11; **9**:52, 59–60
transuranium elements **5**:62, 64
triads, law of **5**:15
triglyceride **8**:48; **9**:14–15, 40–42, 51
triple point **2**:33
triplet code **9**:26
tritium **1**:30–31, 57; **3**:64; **5**:8; **7**:8
tungsten **5**:35; **6**:42–59; **7**:39, 49; **10**:63
turbulence **4**:40

U
ultraviolet radiation **1**:38–39; **4**:28; **10**:51
unit cell **2**:47, 48
universe **1**:4; **4**:39; **5**:4
unsaturated **8**:49; **9**:14
uranium **1**:25, 36, 57, 62–63; **3**:62, 64–65; **5**:5–6, 26, 33, 62, 63–64; **7**:55
decay chain **1**:60–61; **3**:62
urea **8**:5; **9**:46, 48

V
van der Waals forces **1**:51, 52; **3**:18–19
vanadium **5**:31
vapor **2**:30–33, 64; **4**:33, 34, 51; **8**:41
vaporization **1**:8; **2**:30–33
heat of **2**:59, 62–63
vibration **2**:5, 6; **4**:11
vinegar **5**:40; **8**:38, 44, 45

viscosity **2**:25, 26–27, 49; **7**:62
vitamins **6**:56–57, 58; **9**:47–48
volatile **8**:50
volatile liquid **4**:27
volcanoes **1**:6; **5**:49; **6**:39; **7**:16, 47
Volta, Alessandro **3**:50–51
voltage **3**:54
voltaic cell **3**:50–55, 57
volume **1**:7; **2**:18, 20–21
vulcanization **8**:58, 64, 6

W
washing powder **4**:65
water **1**:7, 10, 22–23; **2**:9–10, 24, 25, 27–29, 64–65; **3**:9, 17; **7**:4, 6–7, 10:38–40, 43–51
hard and soft **6**:24; **10**:47, 50
heat capacity **2**:28
heavy **7**:8
hydrogen bonds **1**:52–54
as solvent **1**:15; **2**:29, 36–37; **9**:12; **10**:49–50
water cycle **1**:10; **10**:48, 49
water vapor **1**:7, 8, 10; **2**:31, 63, 64–65; **4**:34; **8**:6; **10**:42, 49
Watson, James **9**:27
wavelength **4**:28–29
wax **2**:5; **9**:12
weathering **10**:44–46, 48, 49
welding **5**:21, 53; **8**:25; **10**:30
Wilkins, Maurice **9**:27
wind power **10**:6–7
Wöhler, Friedrich **8**:5, 7; **9**:46, 48
wood **4**:5, 6; **7**:22–23; **8**:40, 58, 60
work **3**:43; **4**:21, 23

X
X-ray **1**:38–39, 58, 62; **4**:28; **5**:22; **6**:28; **10**:63–65
X-ray crystallography **9**:24
xenon **5**:14, 22, 27, 53; **7**:60–65

Y
yeast **4**:57; **8**:40, 45; **9**:36
yttrium **5**:28, 31

Z
zeolite **8**:27, 28
zinc **3**:18, 20, 26, 28; **5**:12, 15, 39–41; **6**:6, 13, 44–59; **10**:32, 35
zirconium **6**:42–59